WINTER BRUCE HALEY

Daylight

20 YEARS

Cofounders: Taj Forer and Michael Itkoff
Creative Director: Ursula Damm
Copy Editor: Gabrielle Fastman

Digital Imaging by John O'Connor

ISBN: 978-1-954119-04-8

Printed by Ofset Yapimevi, Turkey

Daylight Books
E-mail: info@daylightbooks.org
Web: www.daylightbooks.org

Often in winter I think of those questions that came to Job from the whirlwind:

From whose womb does the ice come forth, and who has given birth to the frost of heaven when the waters become hard as stone, when the surface of the deep is frozen?

In my mind's eye it is all Blakean imagery and thunderous voice, trailing in its wake a near echo from Christina Rossetti: "Earth stood hard as iron, water like a stone."

My ideal world is a perpetual cycle of autumn and winter, burnished gold followed by a canvas of white, over and over.

This book represents my fascination with the arc of winter, and the wild variations of ice and snow found among both the man-altered landscapes and the untouched places of the region that I call home.

In the opening image it is October along Dismal Creek, and in the golden grasses may be seen the scattered remnants of an early but quickly disappearing snow. Before long this entire area will be buried in white for month after month.

In the final image it is April on the edge of Massacre Rim, looking westward across Long Valley and over the Hays Canyon Range, with snow's last redoubt in the far distance of the Warner Mountains.

Between those two images is a twisting pathway through the heart of my winter, into the stillness of a dormant world.

—Bruce Haley, December 2022

It is a winter's tale
That the snow blind twilight ferries over the lakes
And floating fields from the farm in the cup of the vales,
Gliding windless through the hand folded flakes,
The pale breath of cattle at the stealthy sail,

And the stars falling cold,
And the smell of hay in the snow, and the far owl
Warning among the folds, and the frozen hold
Flocked with the sheep white smoke of the farm house cowl
In the river wended vales where the tale was told.

—Dylan Thomas, "A Winter's Tale"

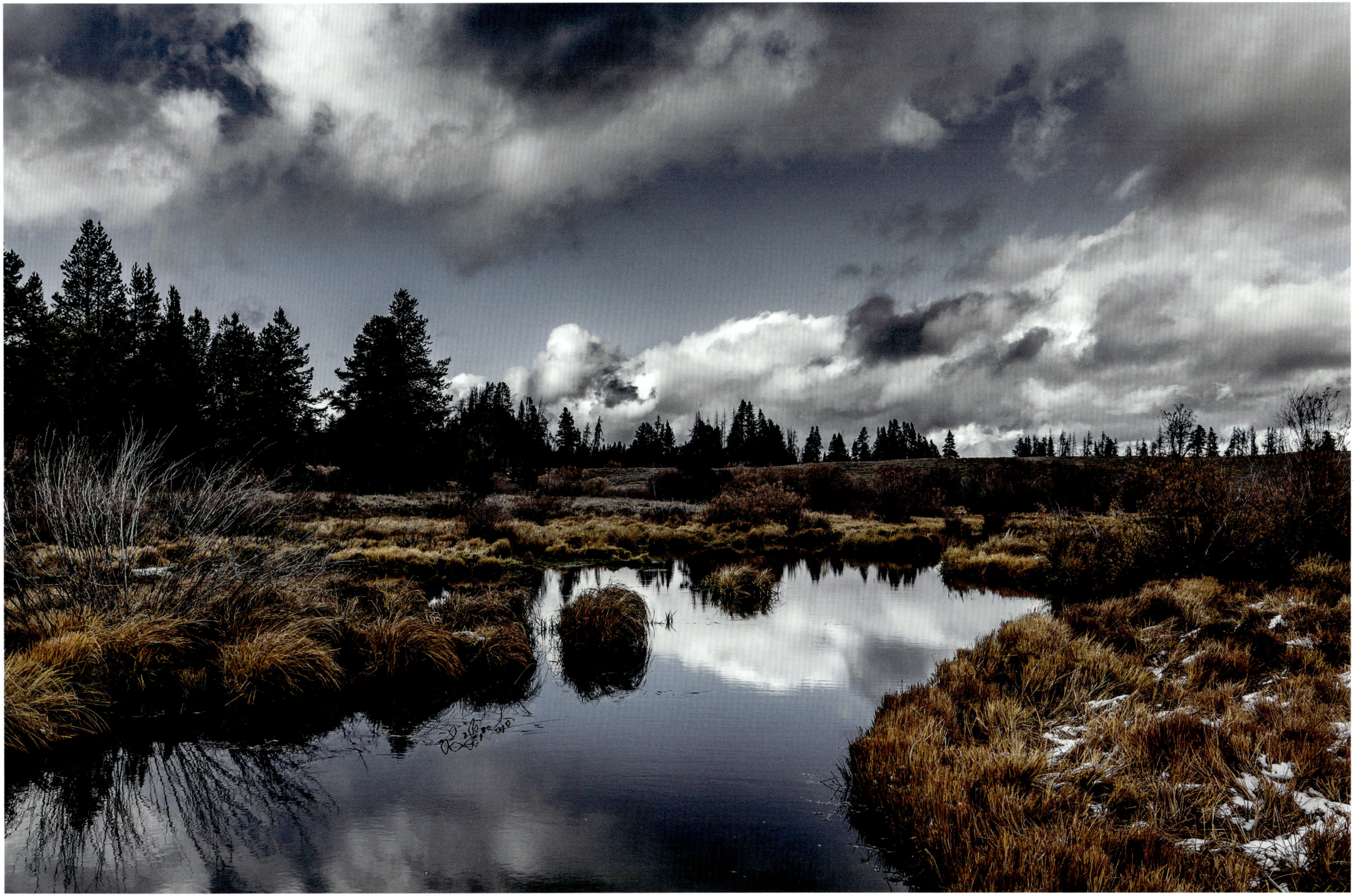

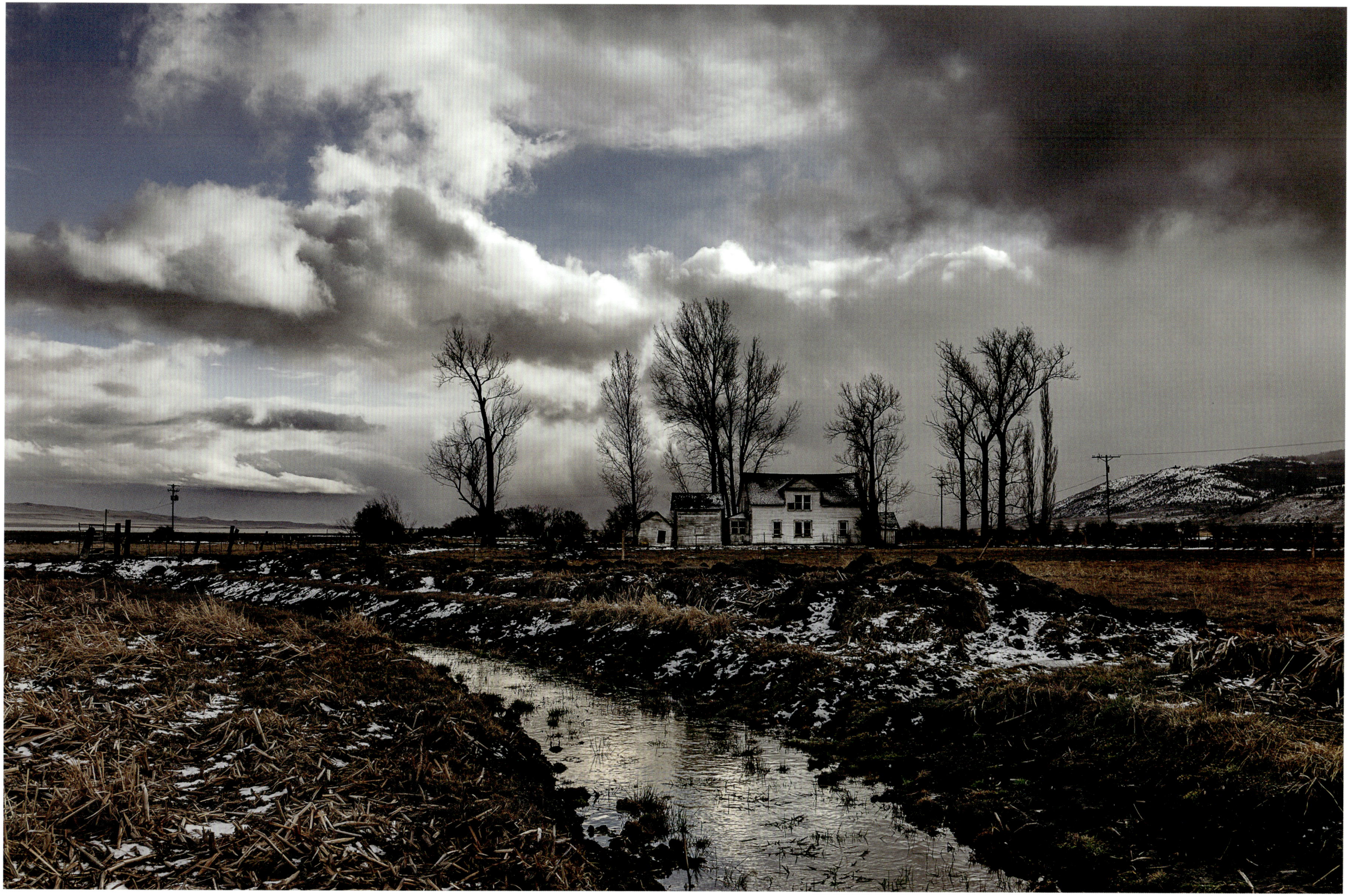

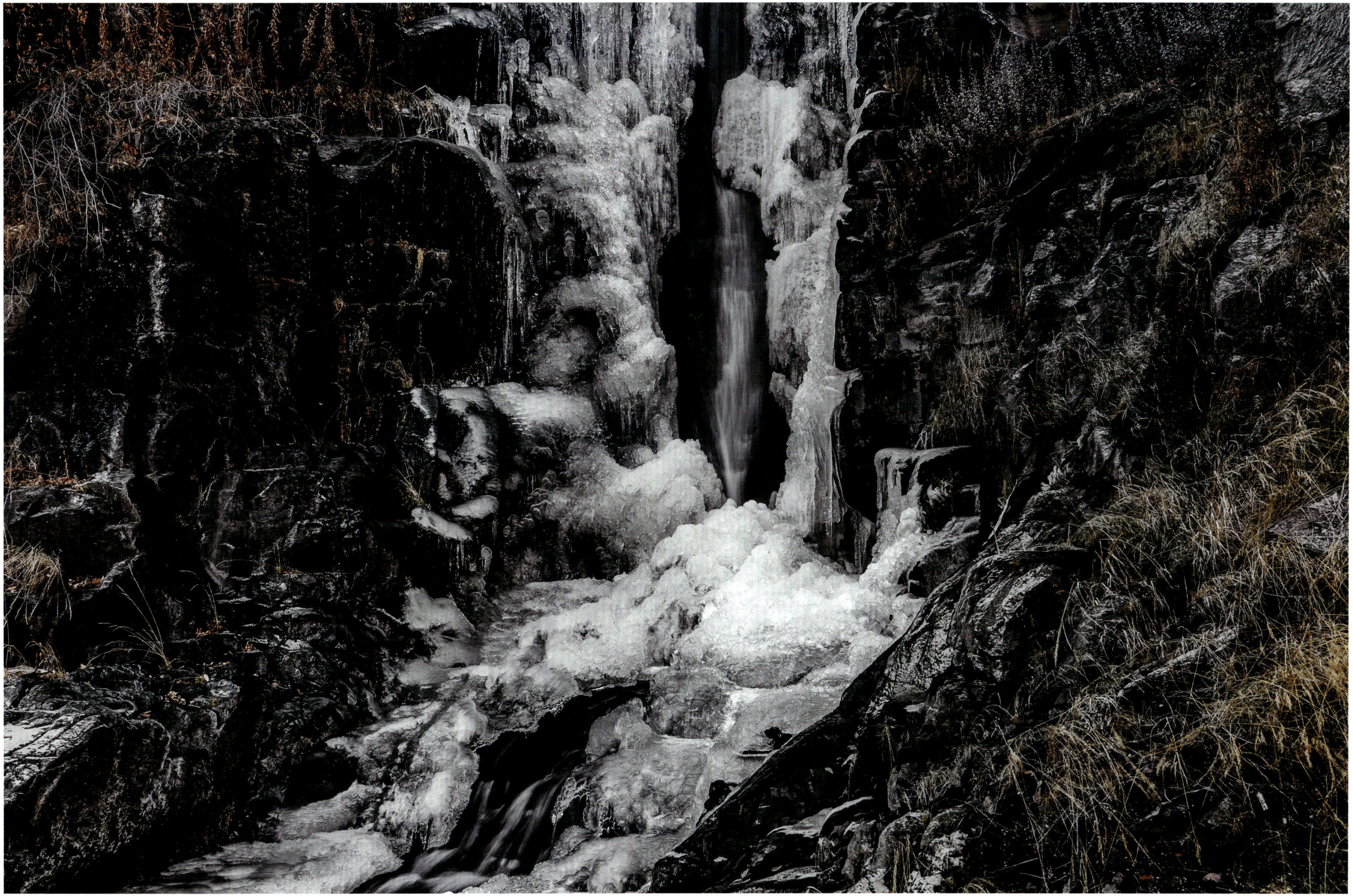

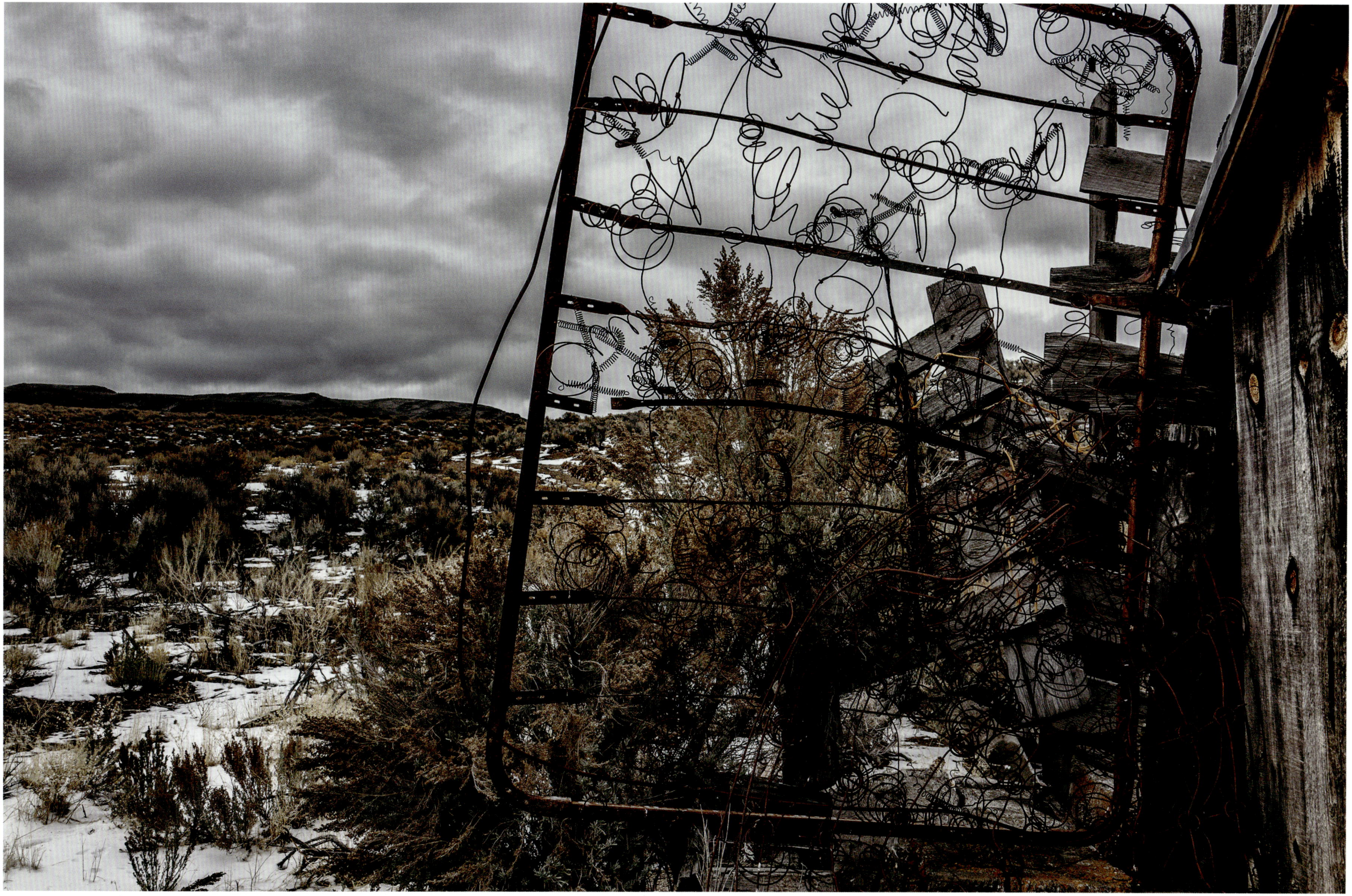

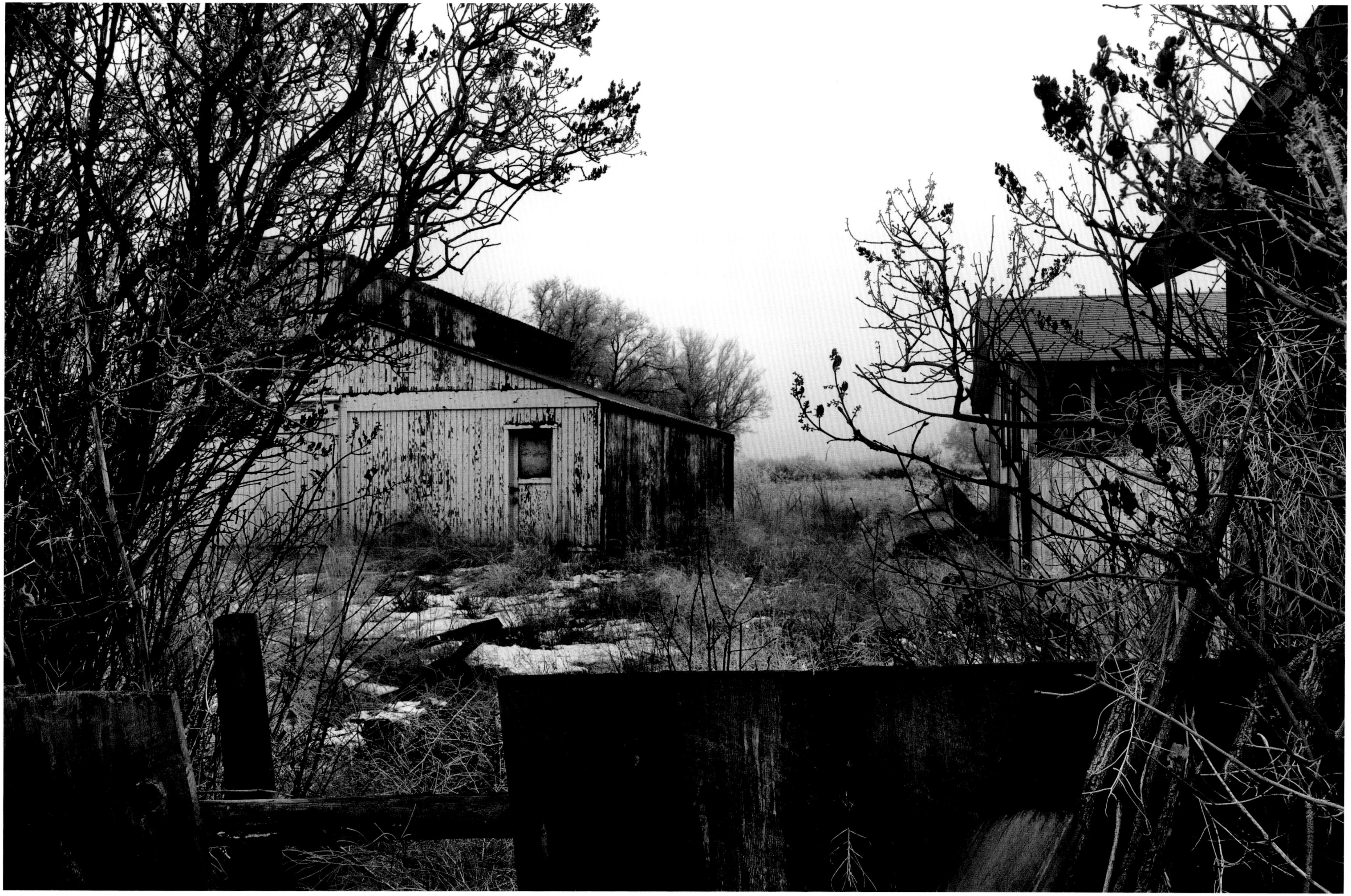

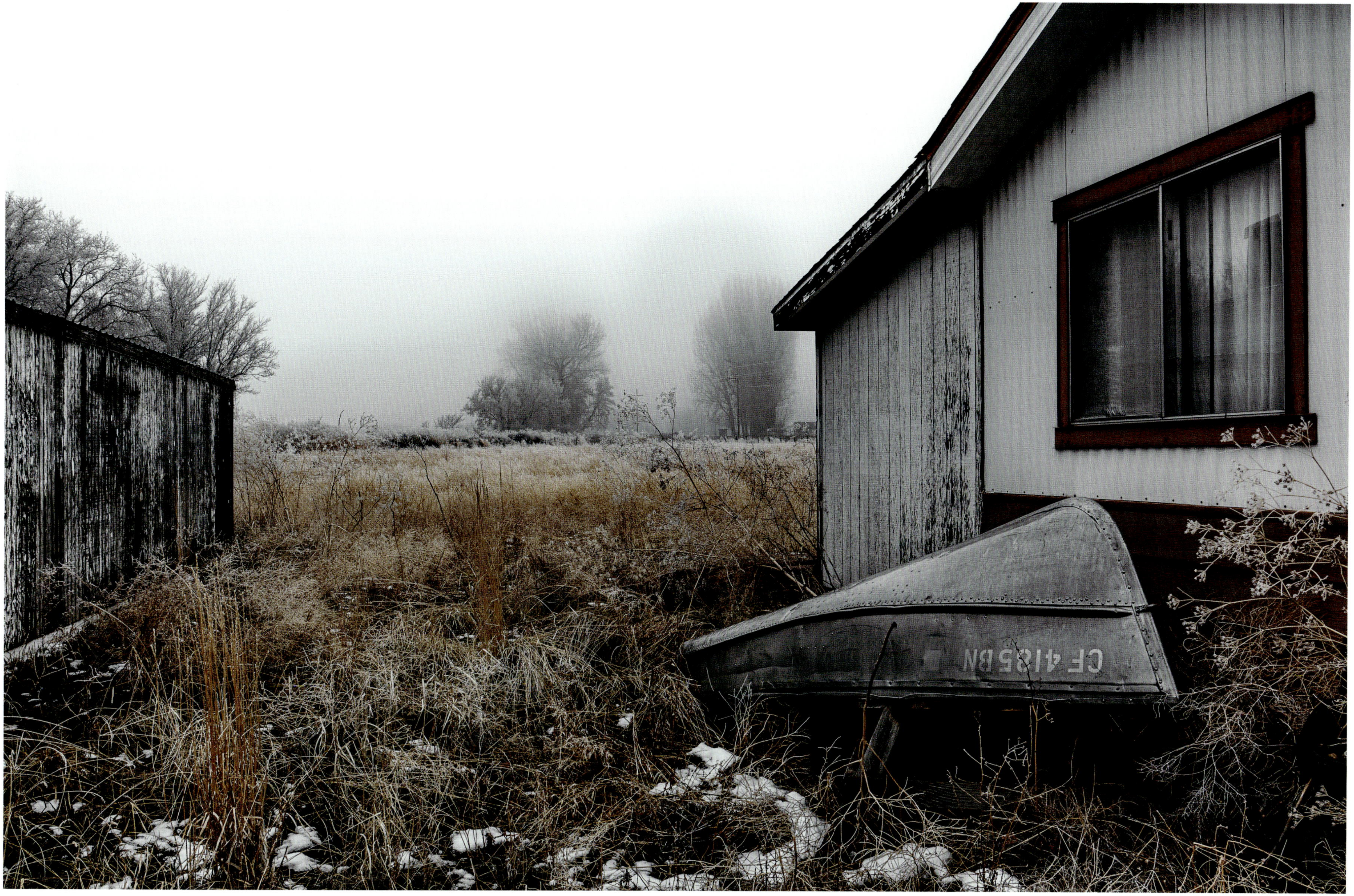
CF 4185 BN

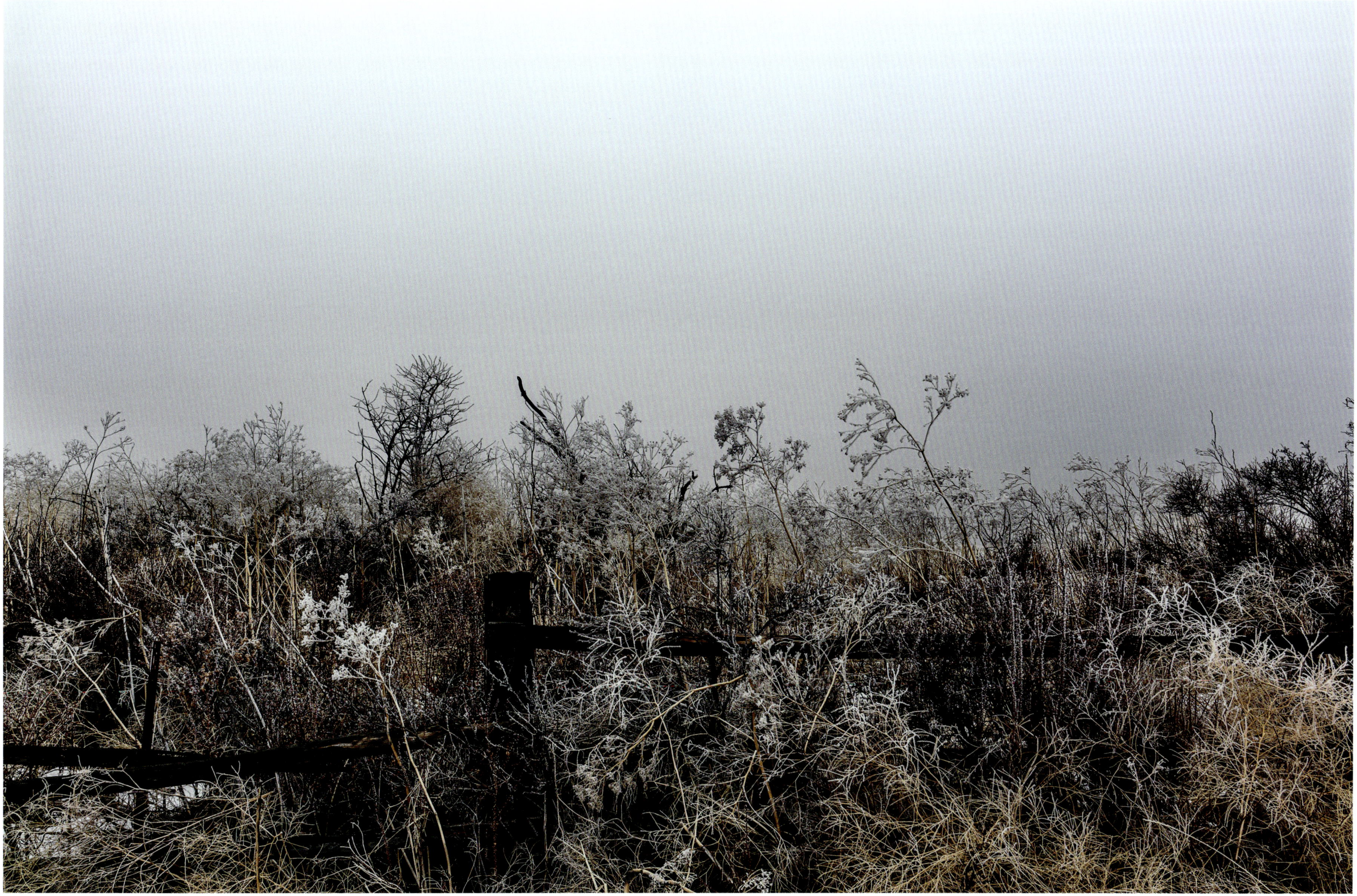

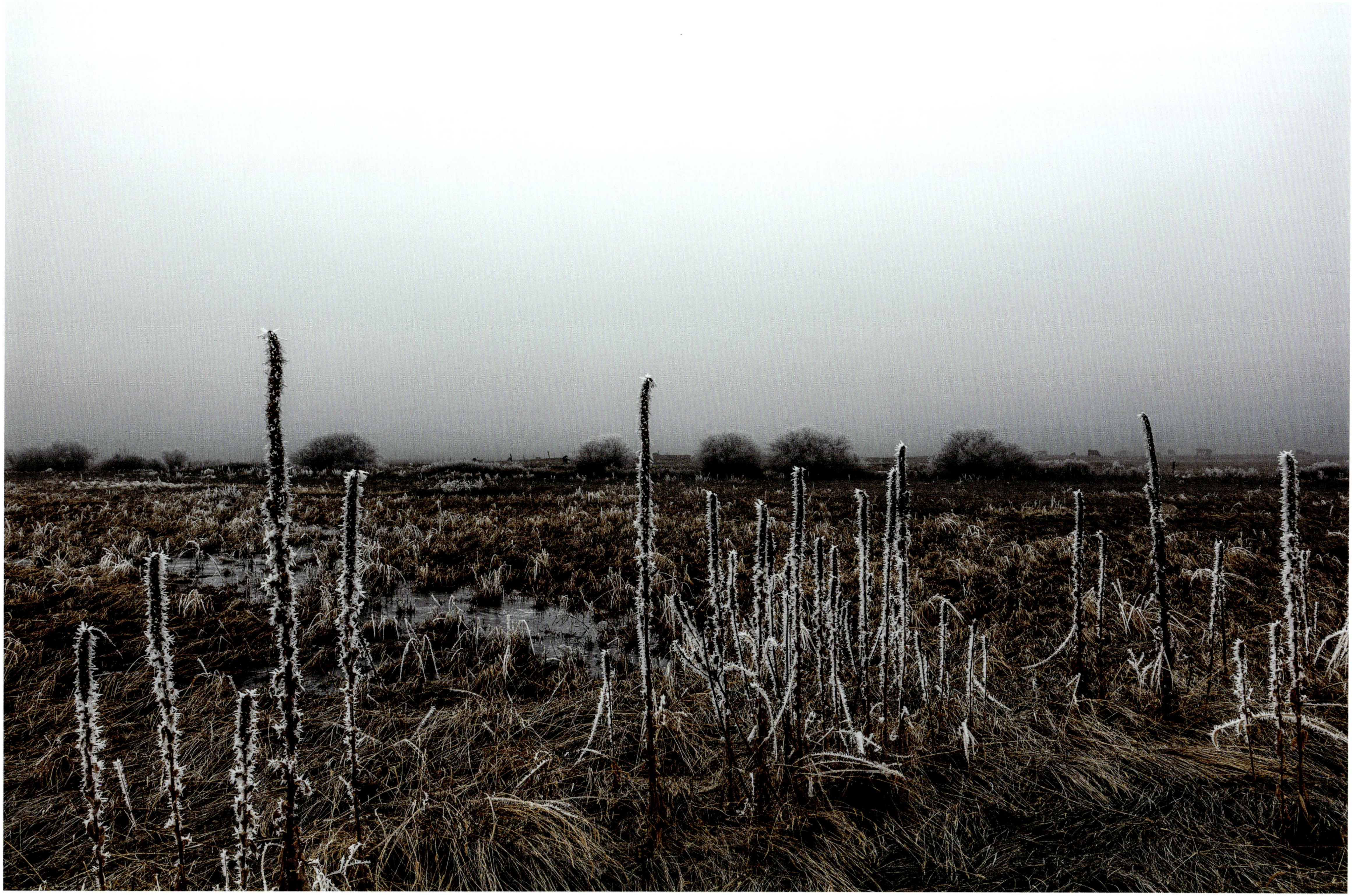

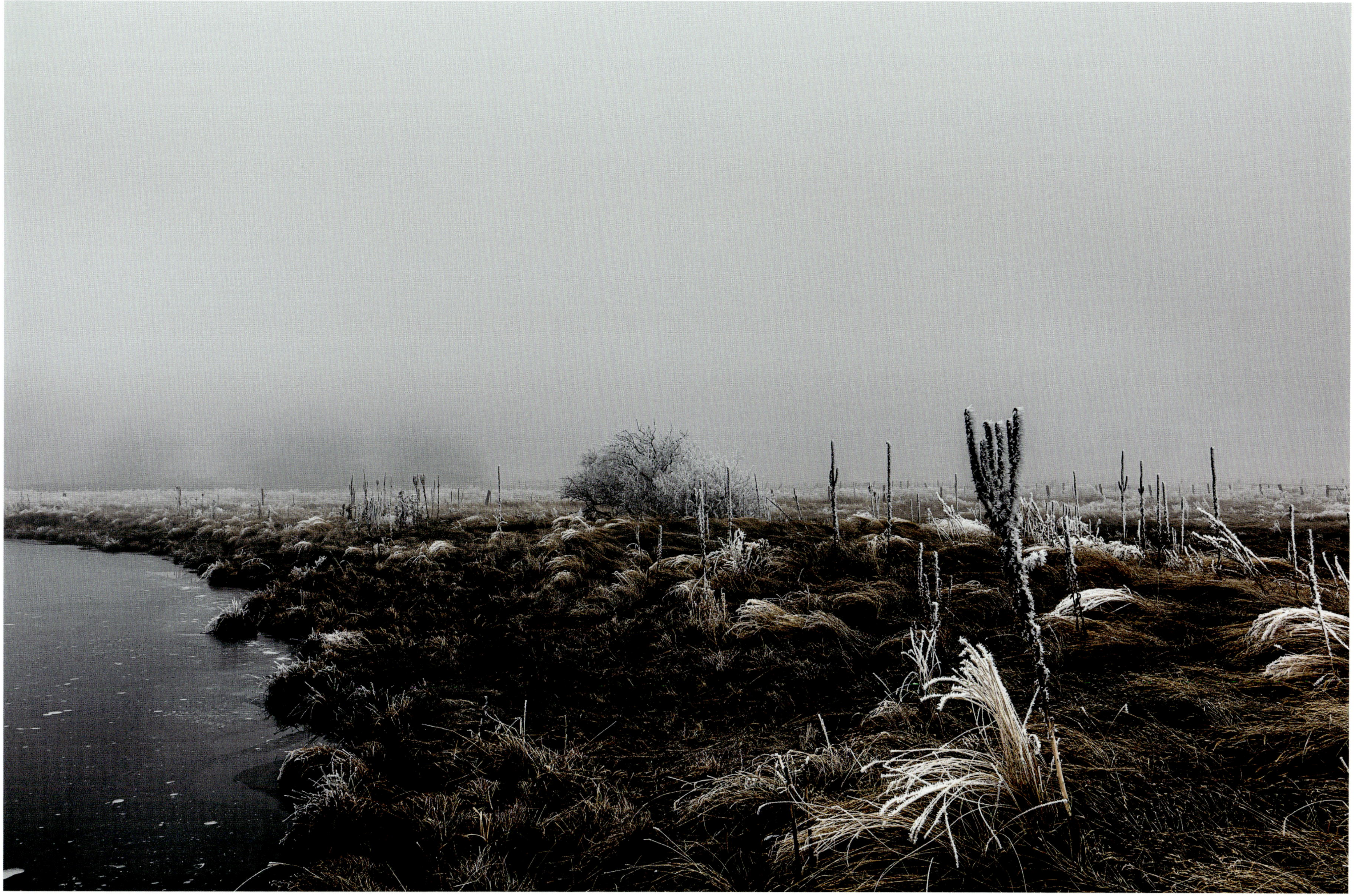

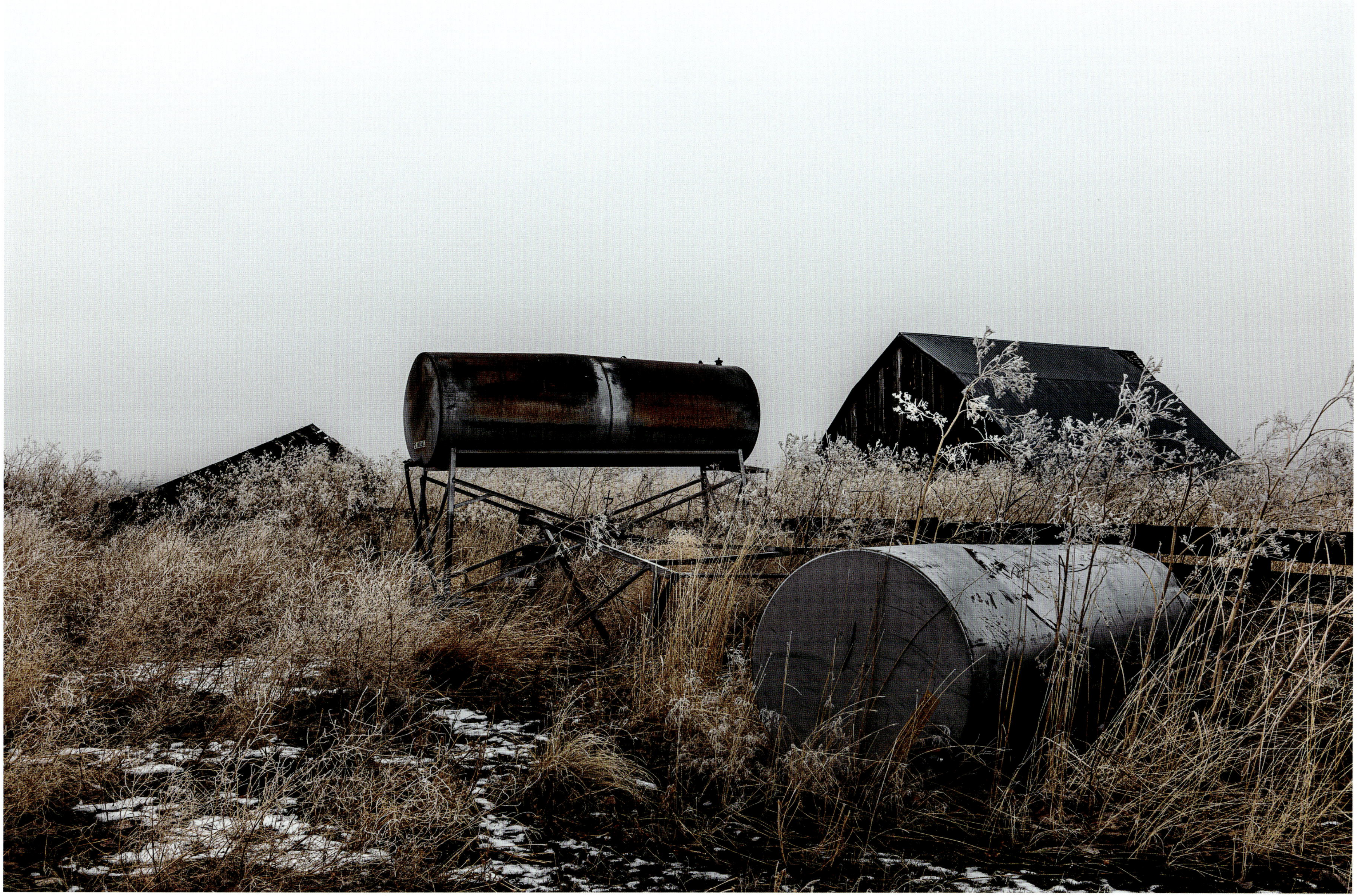

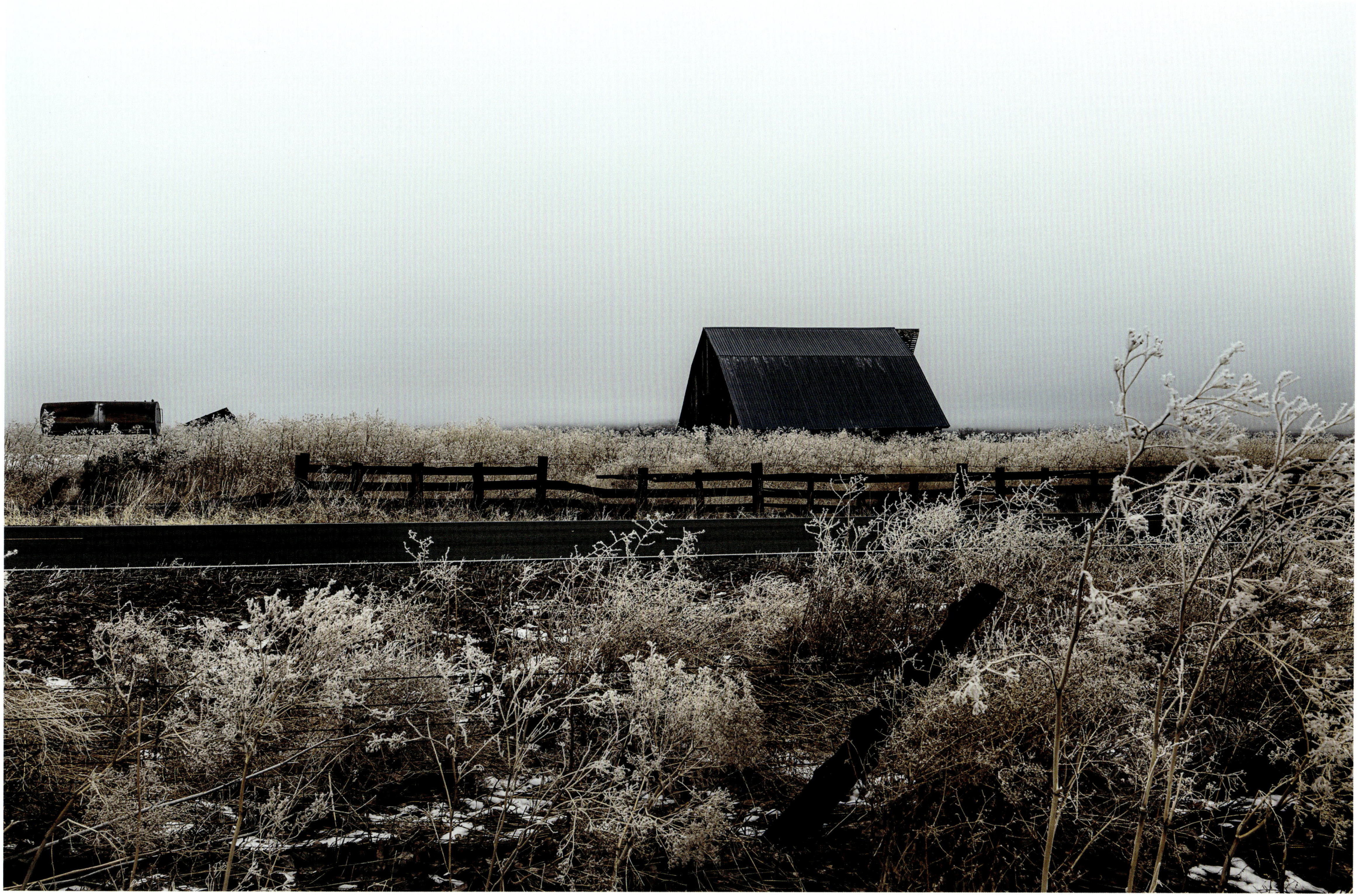

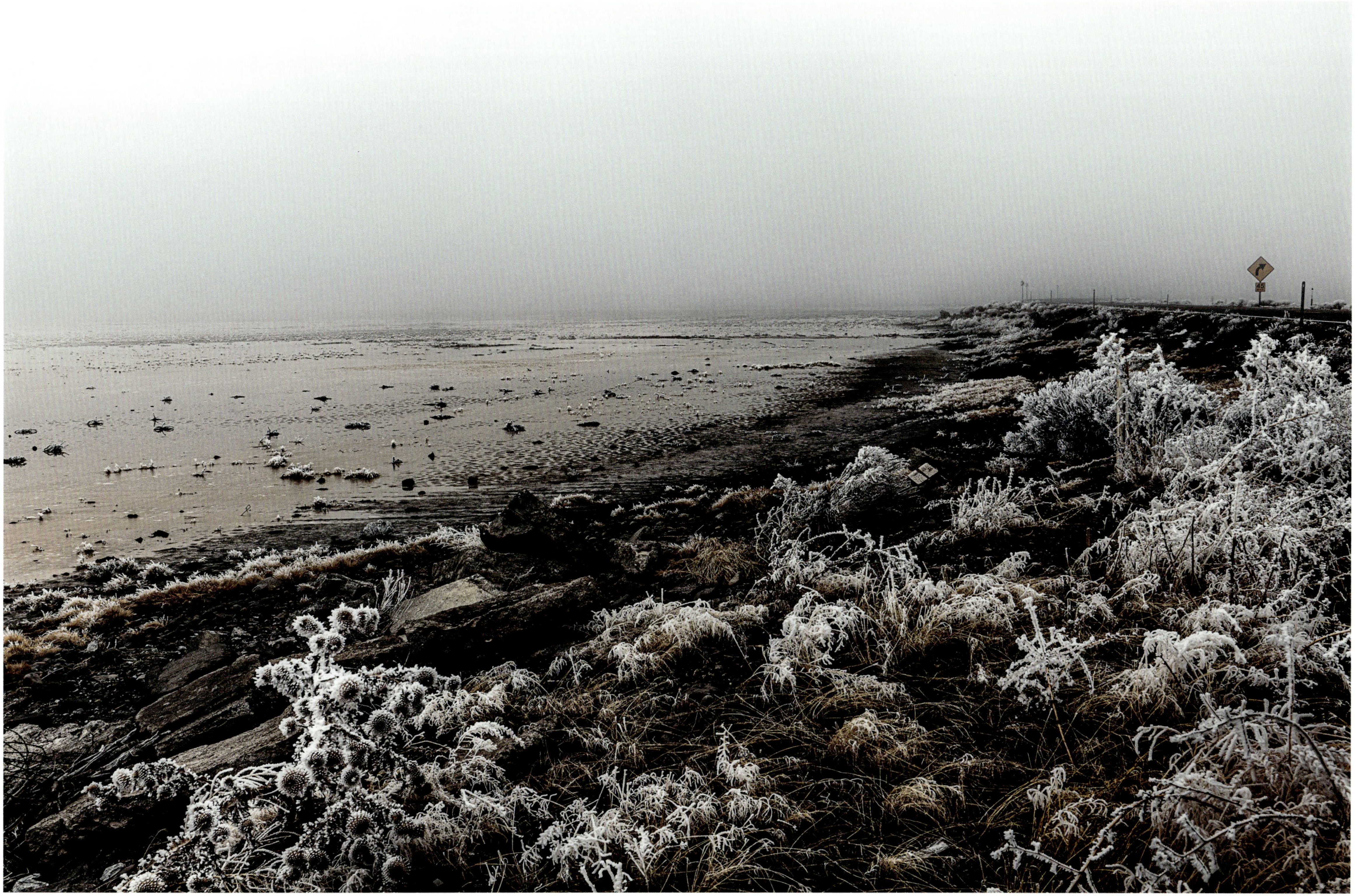

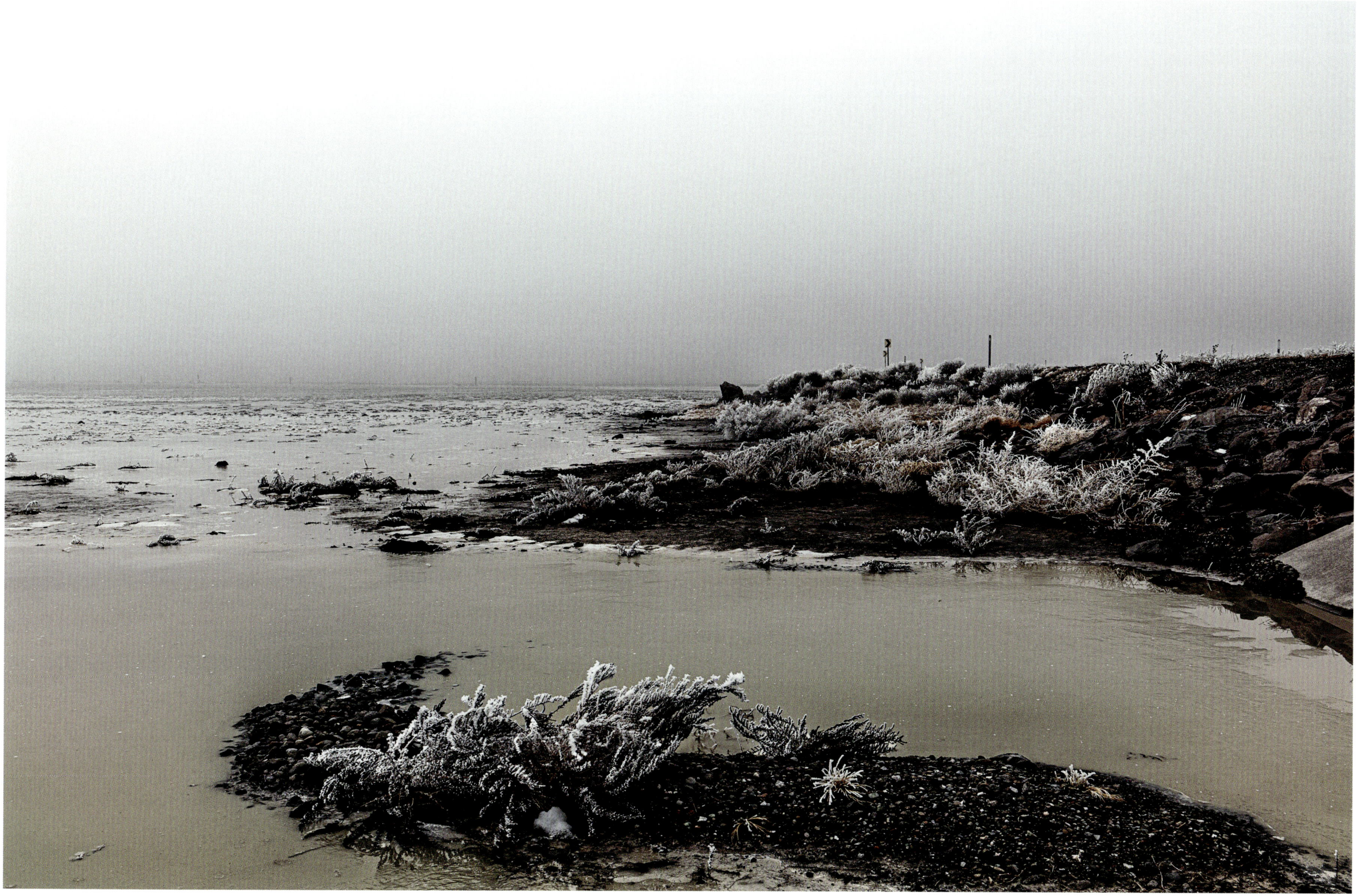

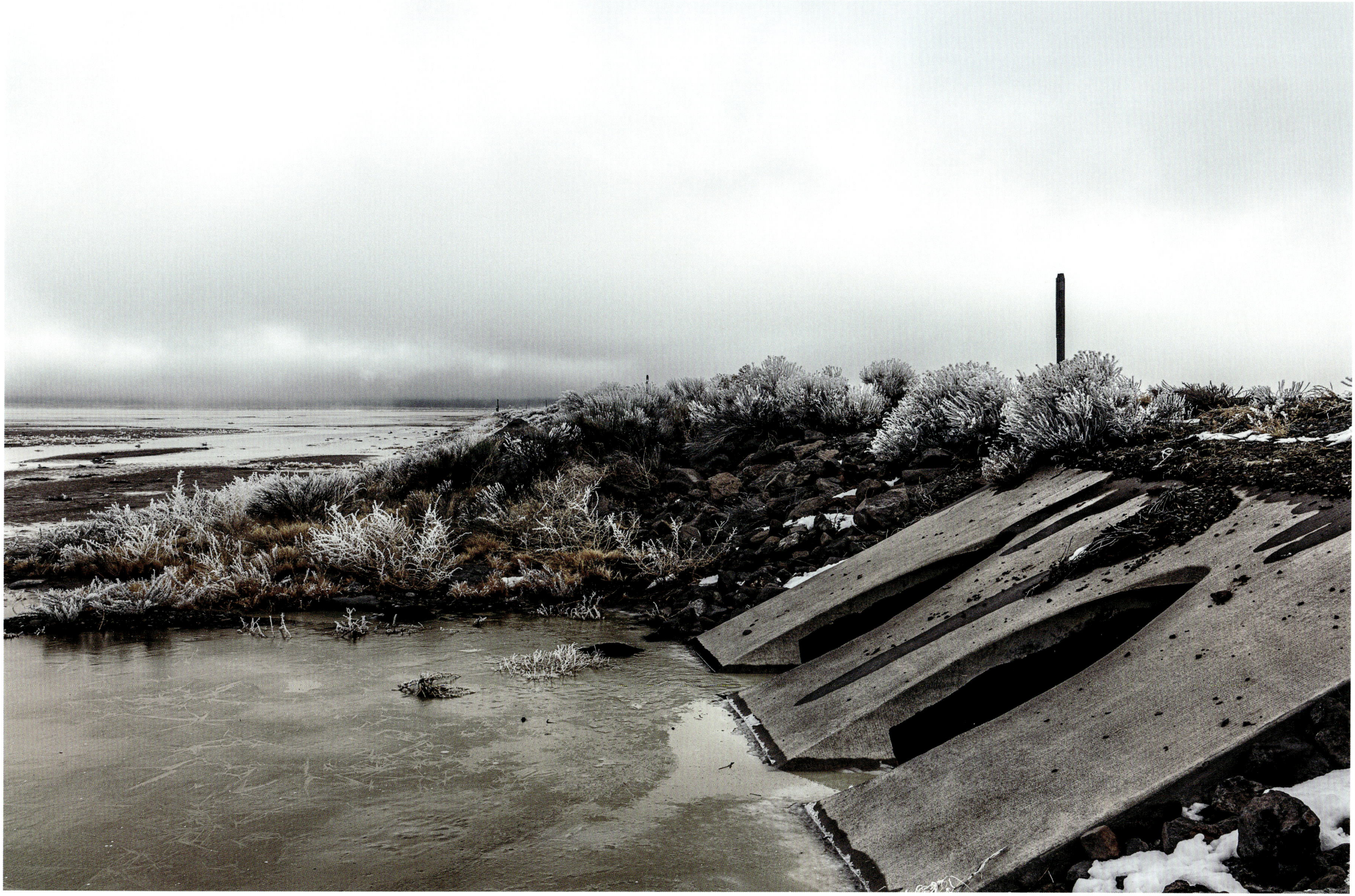

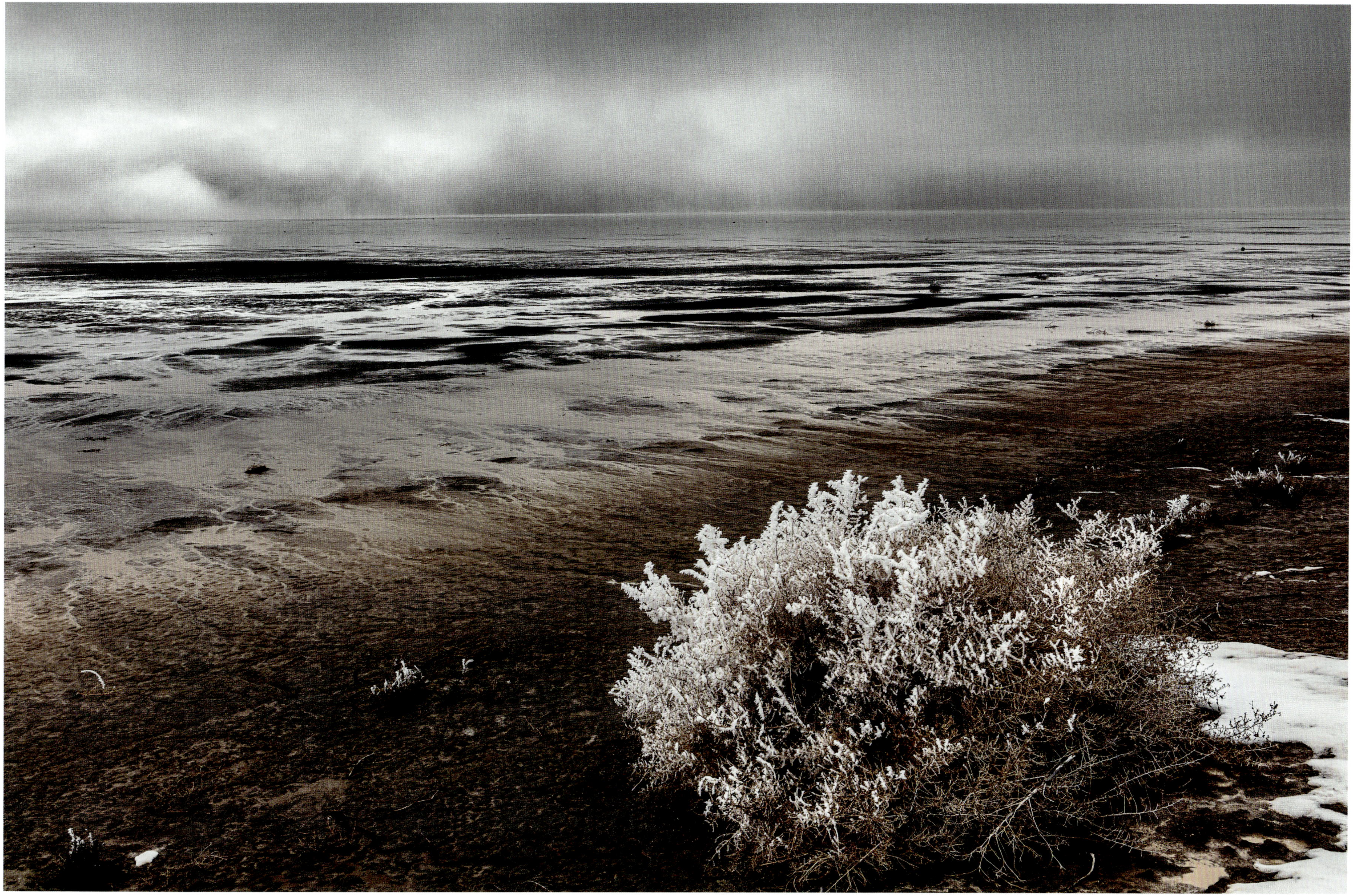

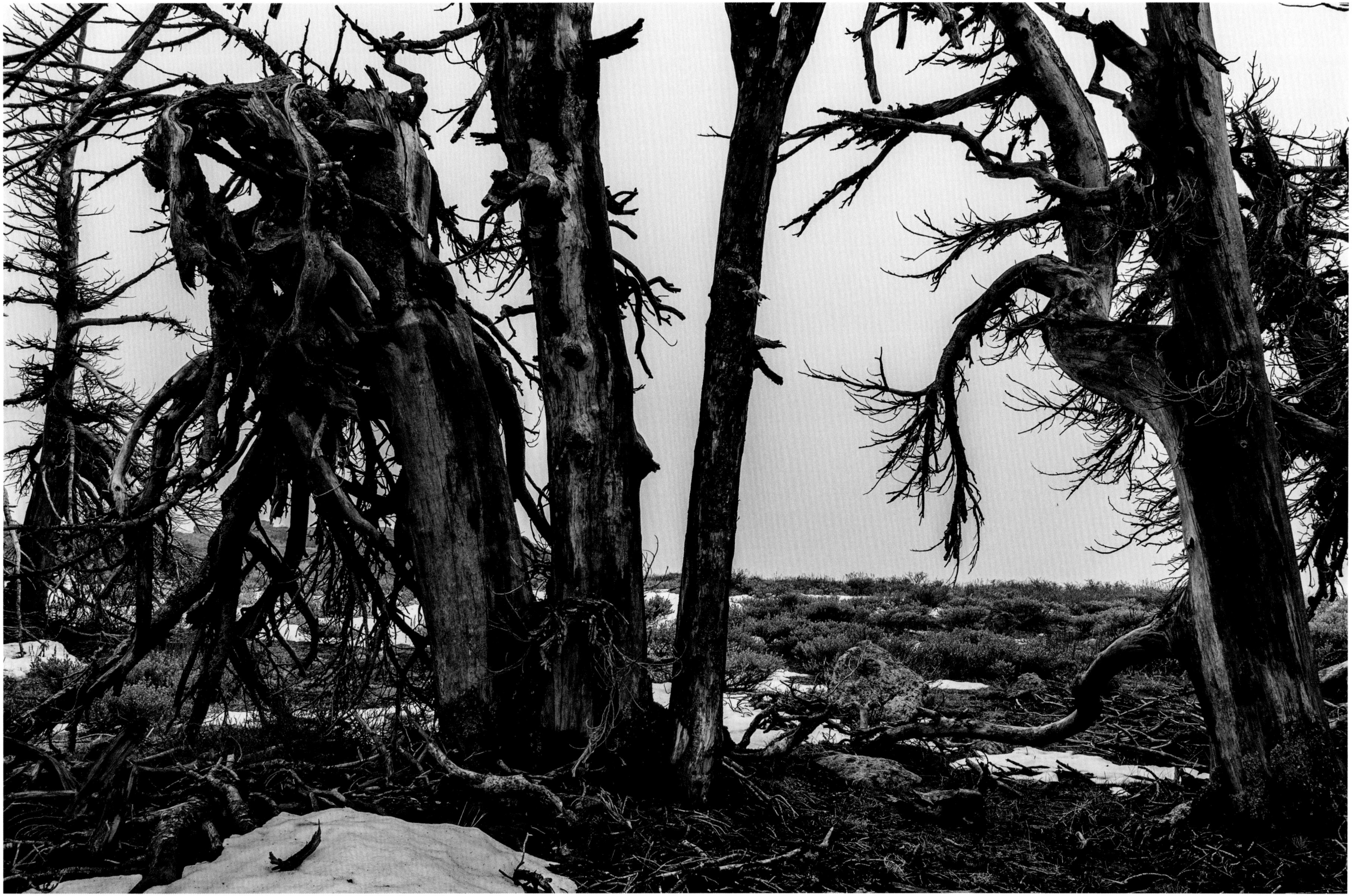

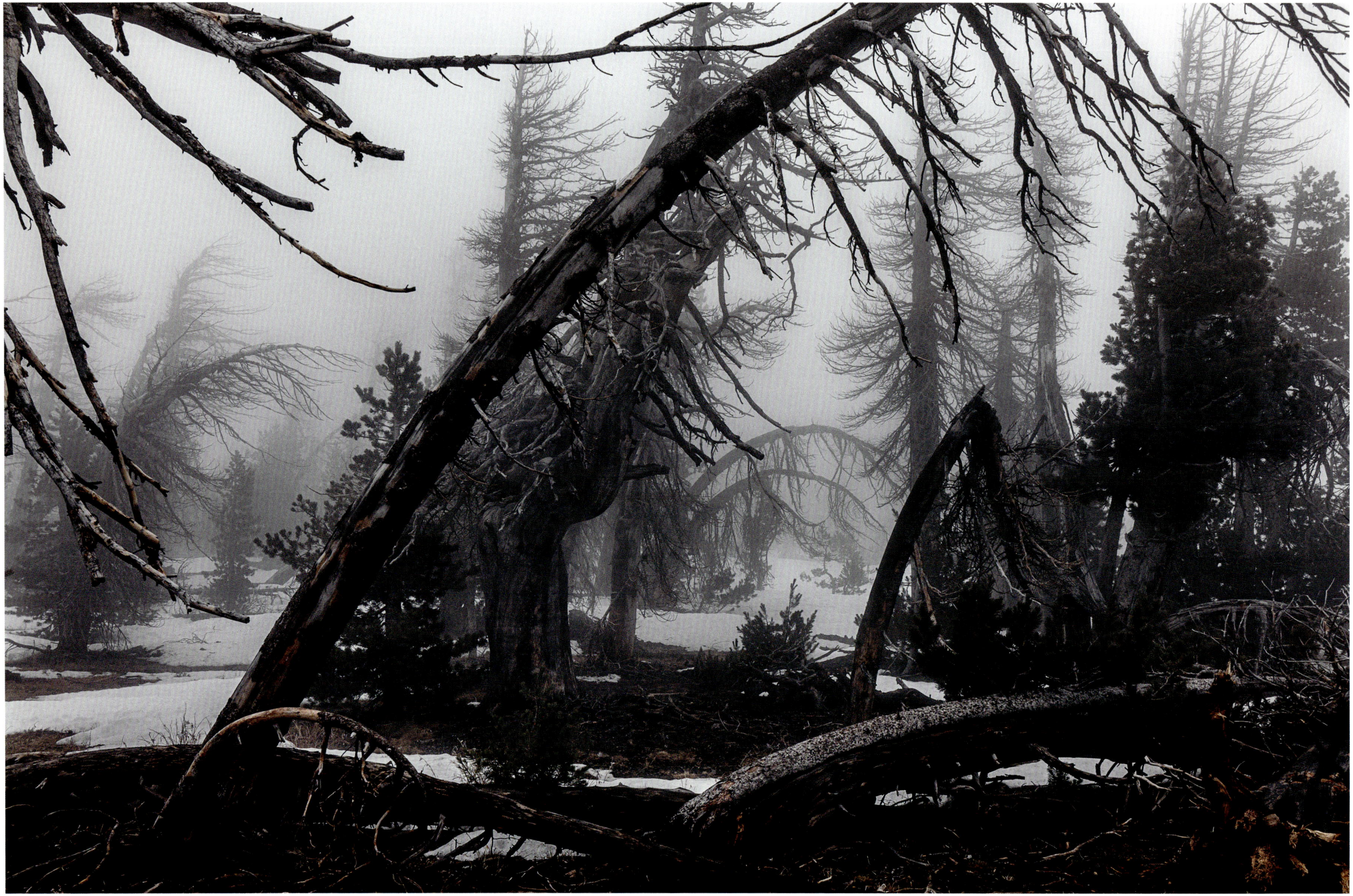

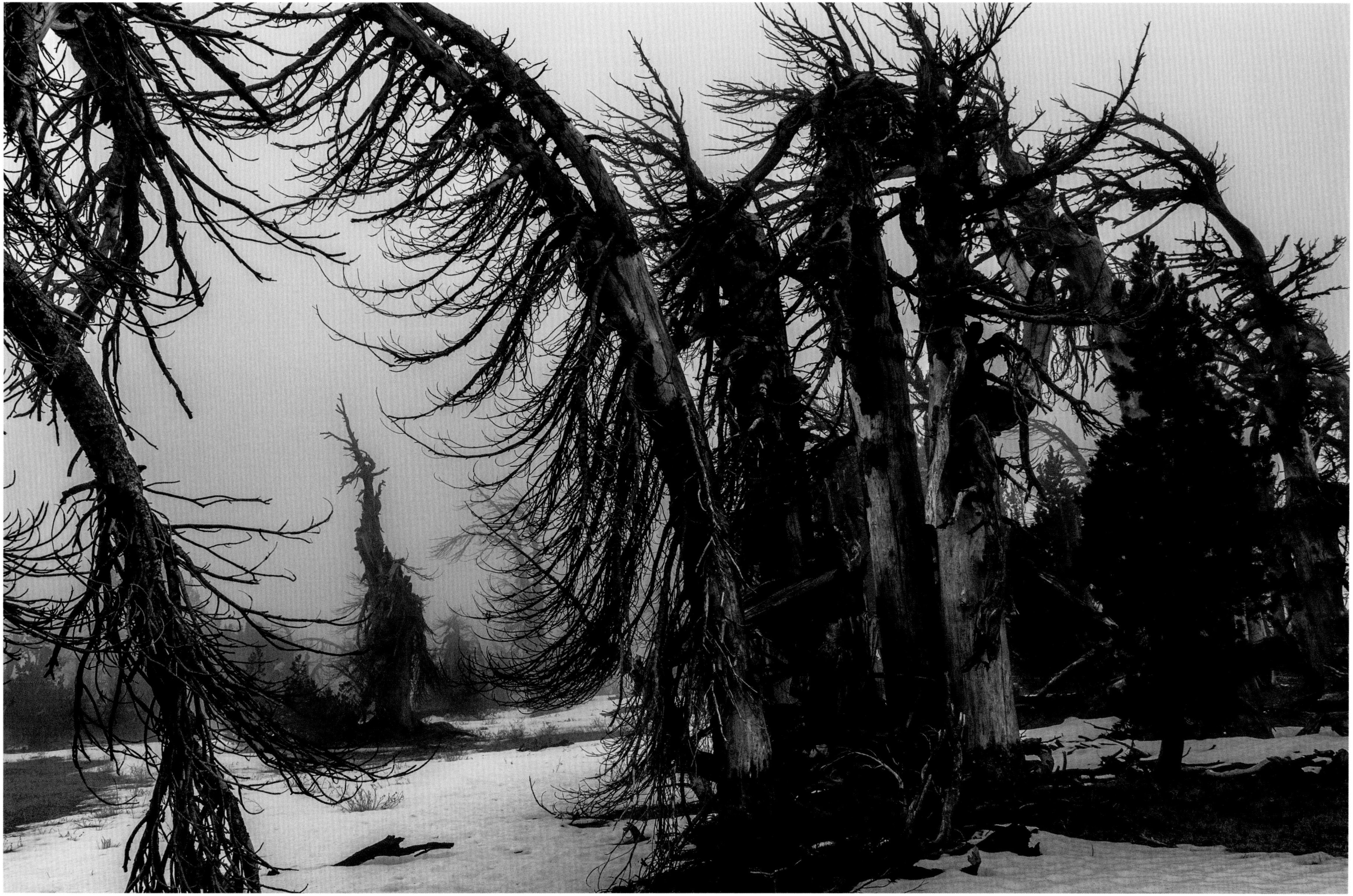

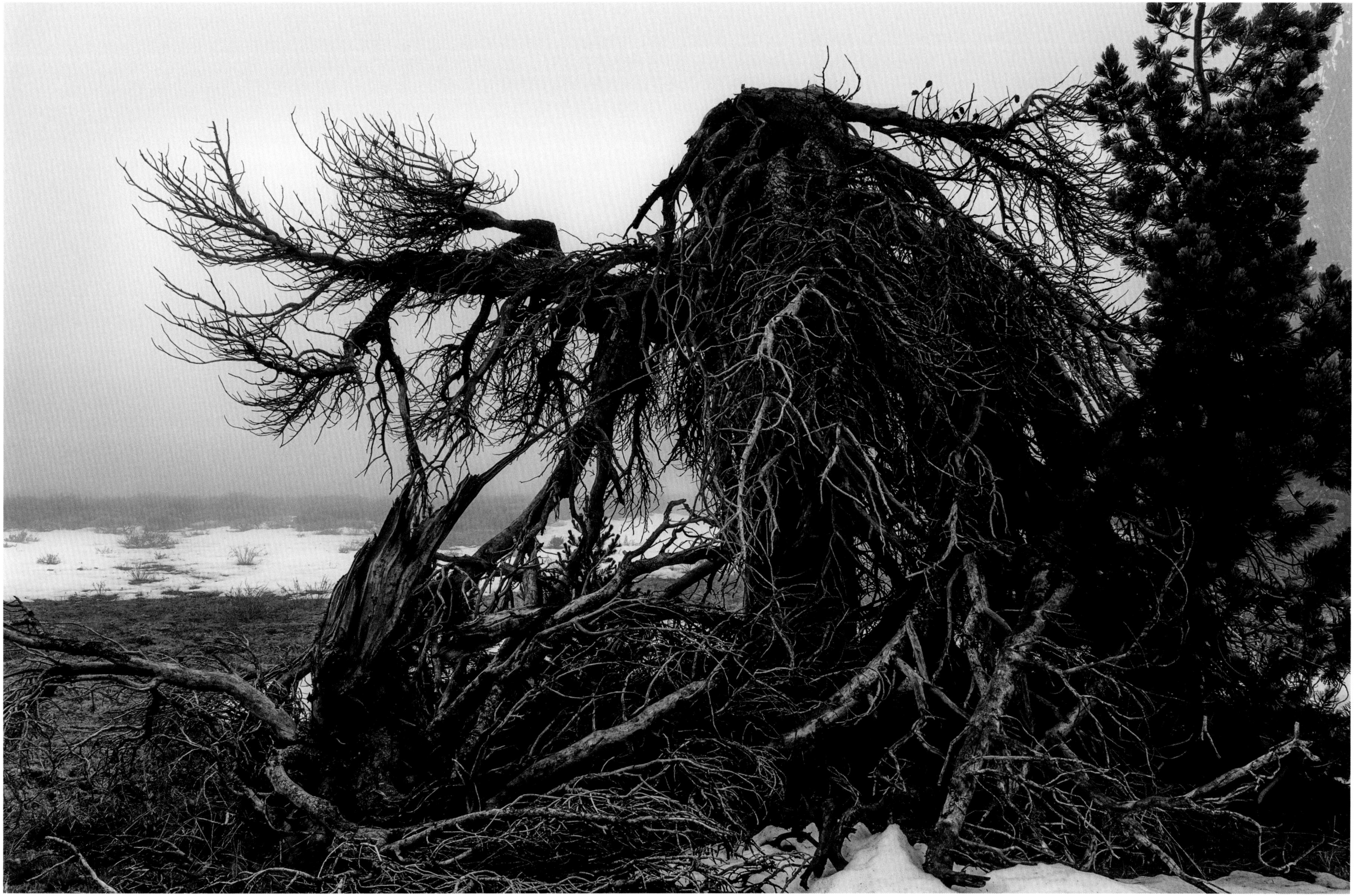

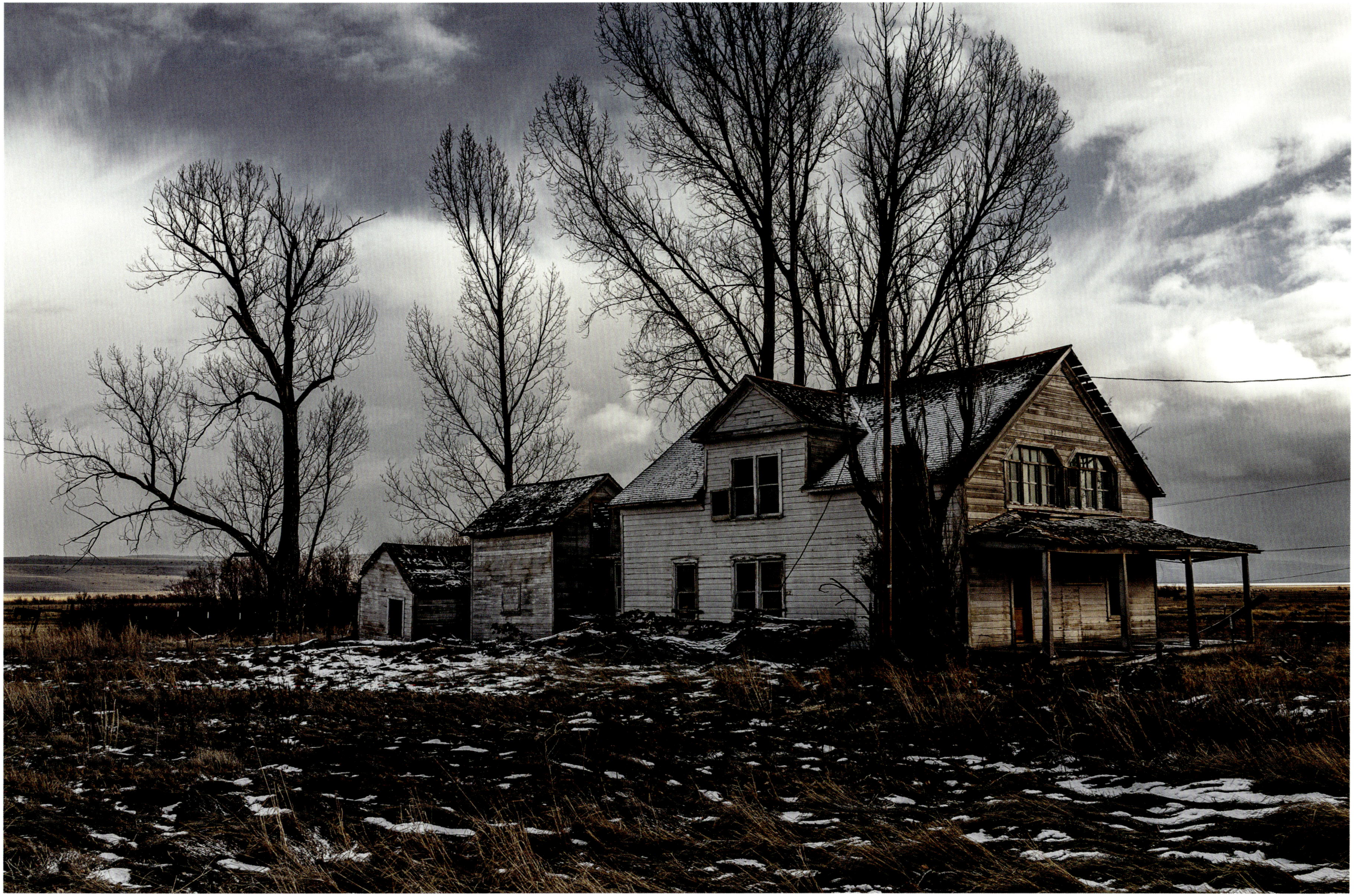

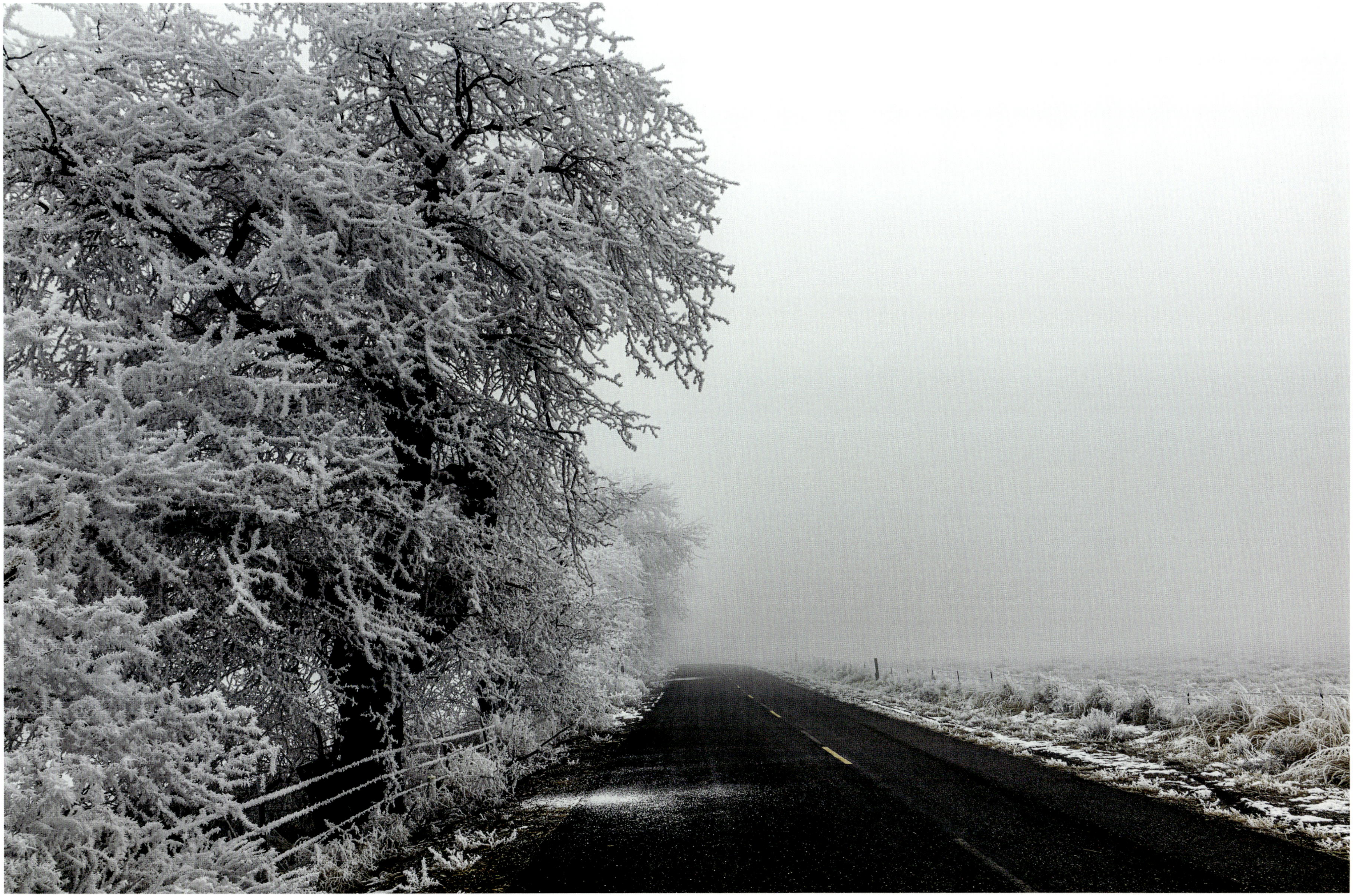

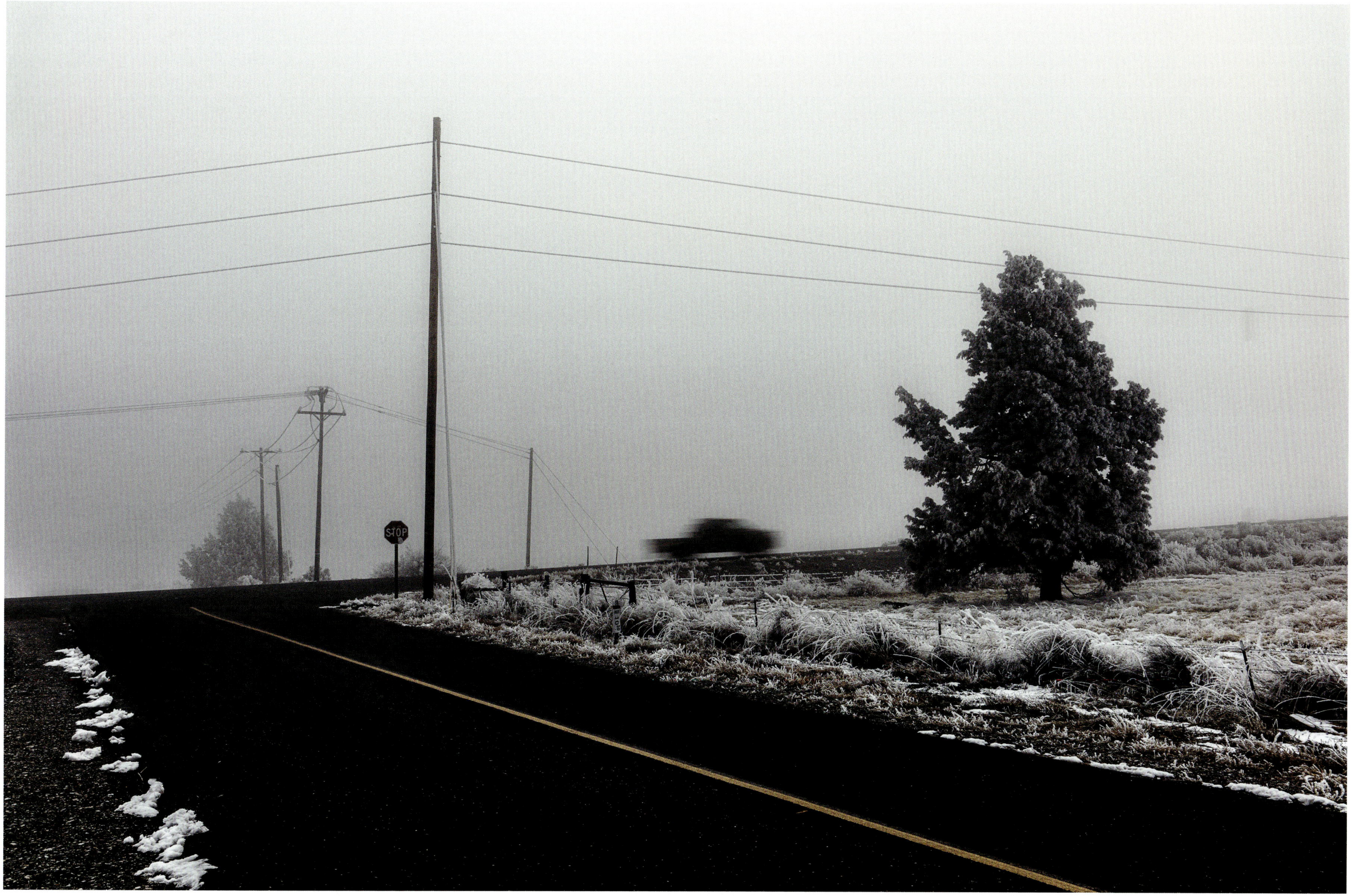
STOP

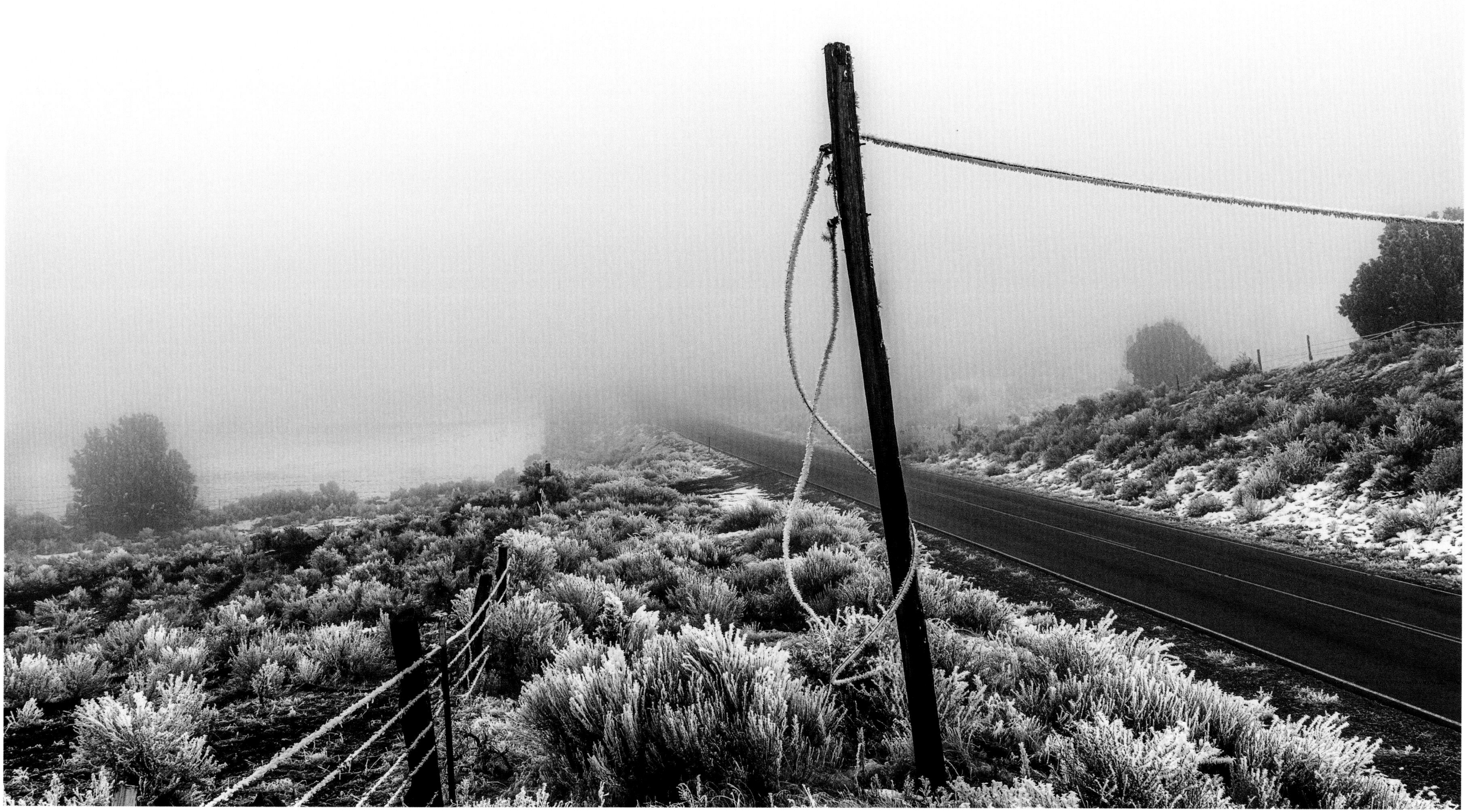

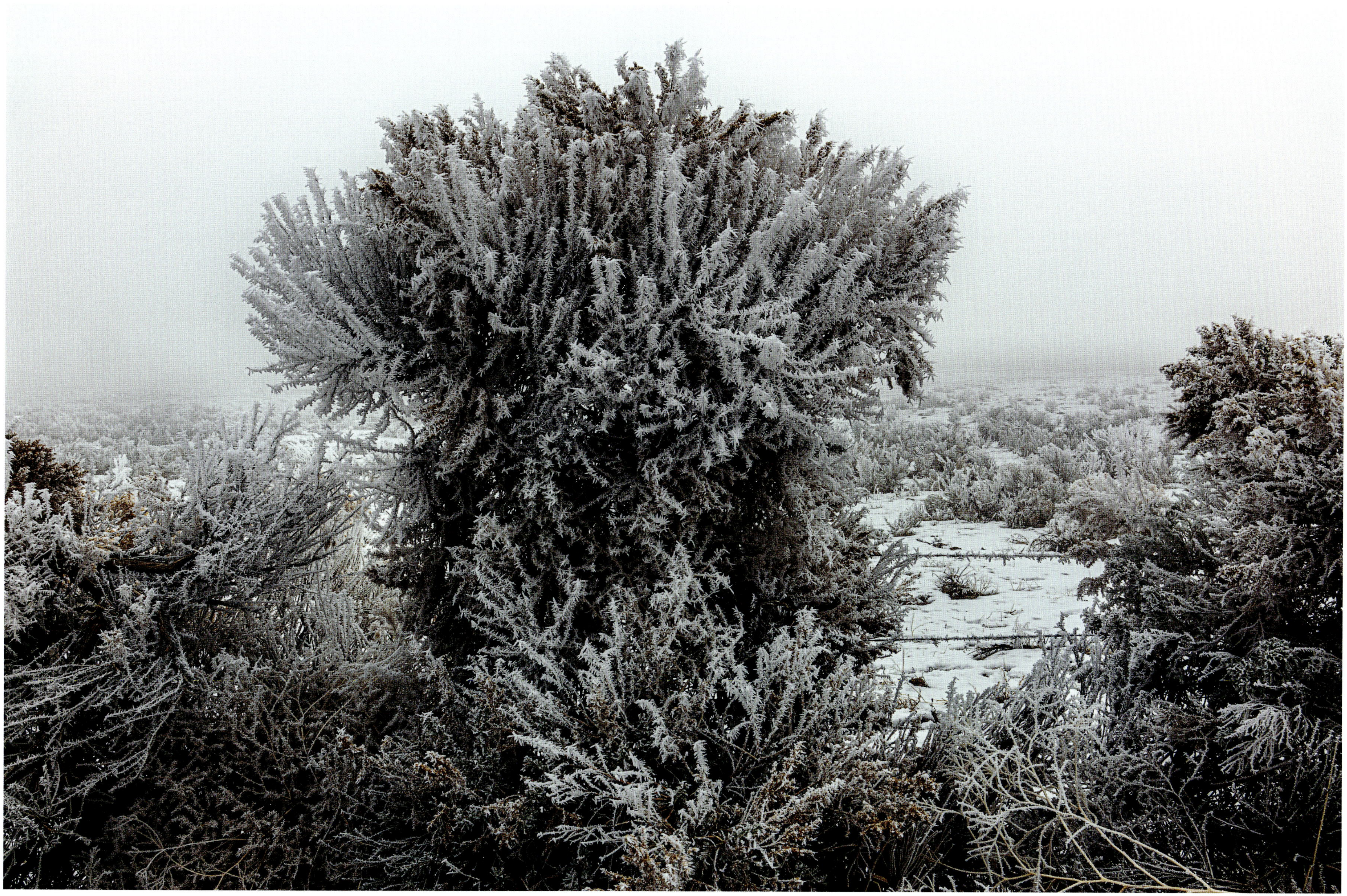

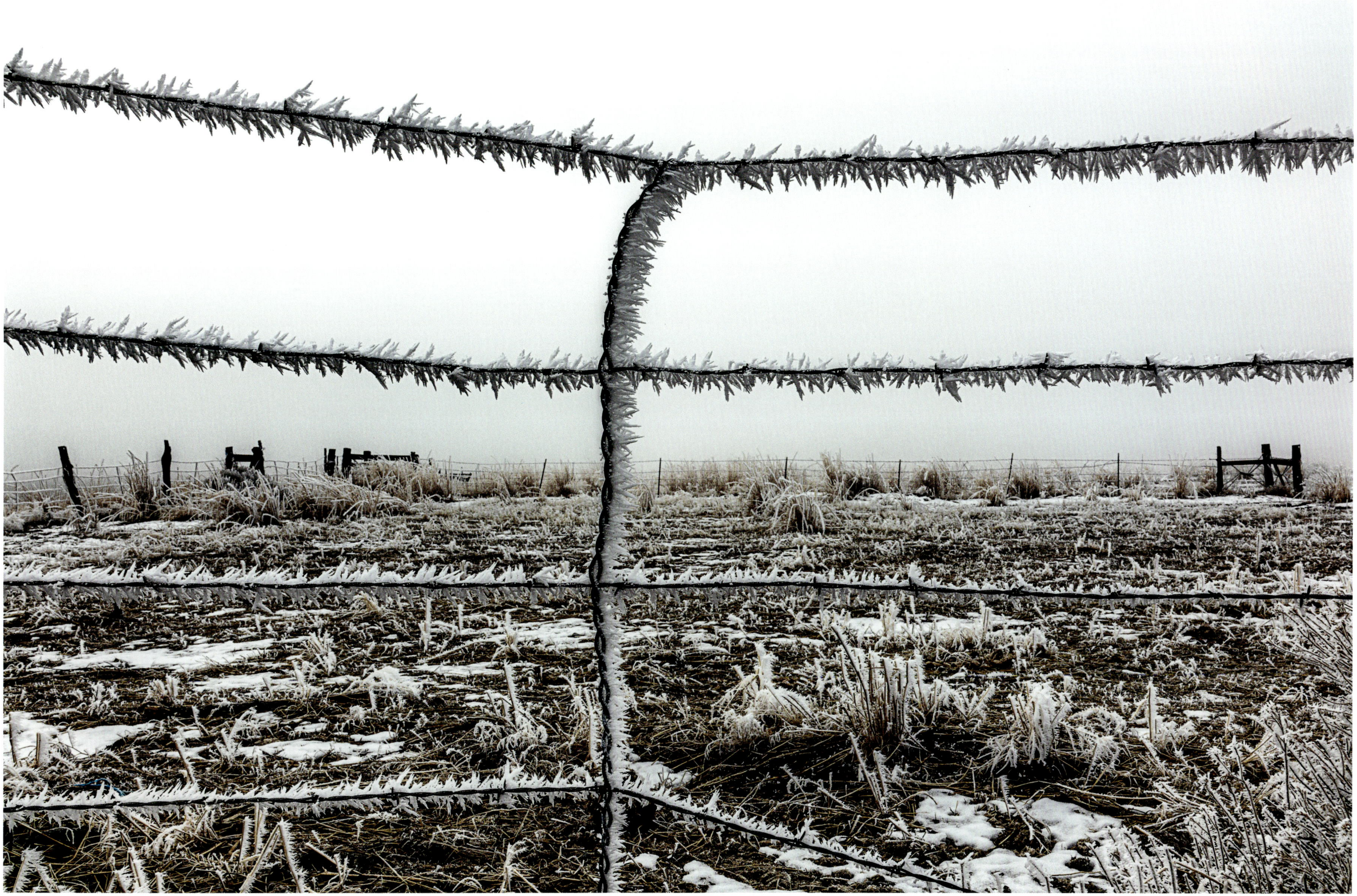

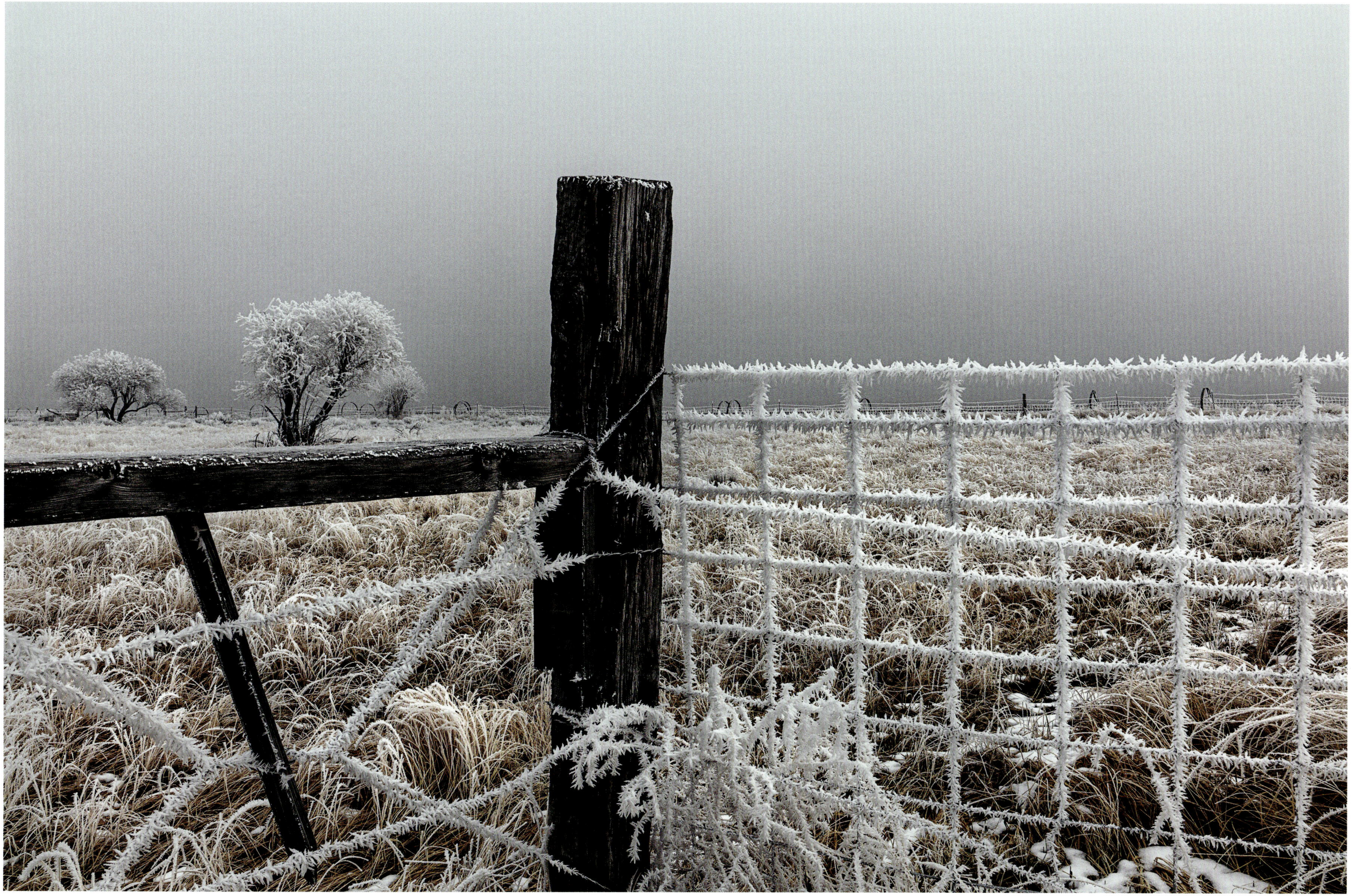

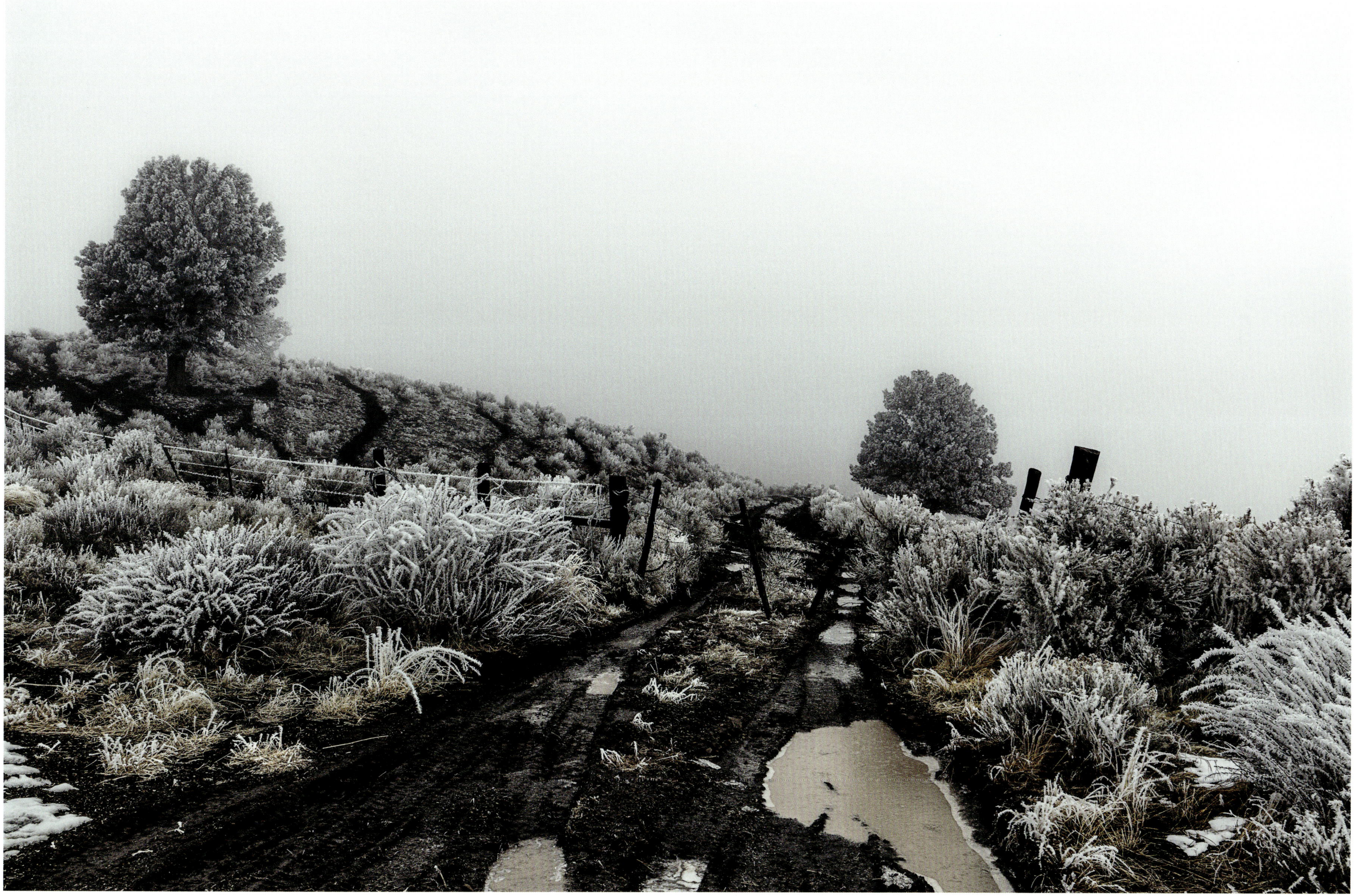

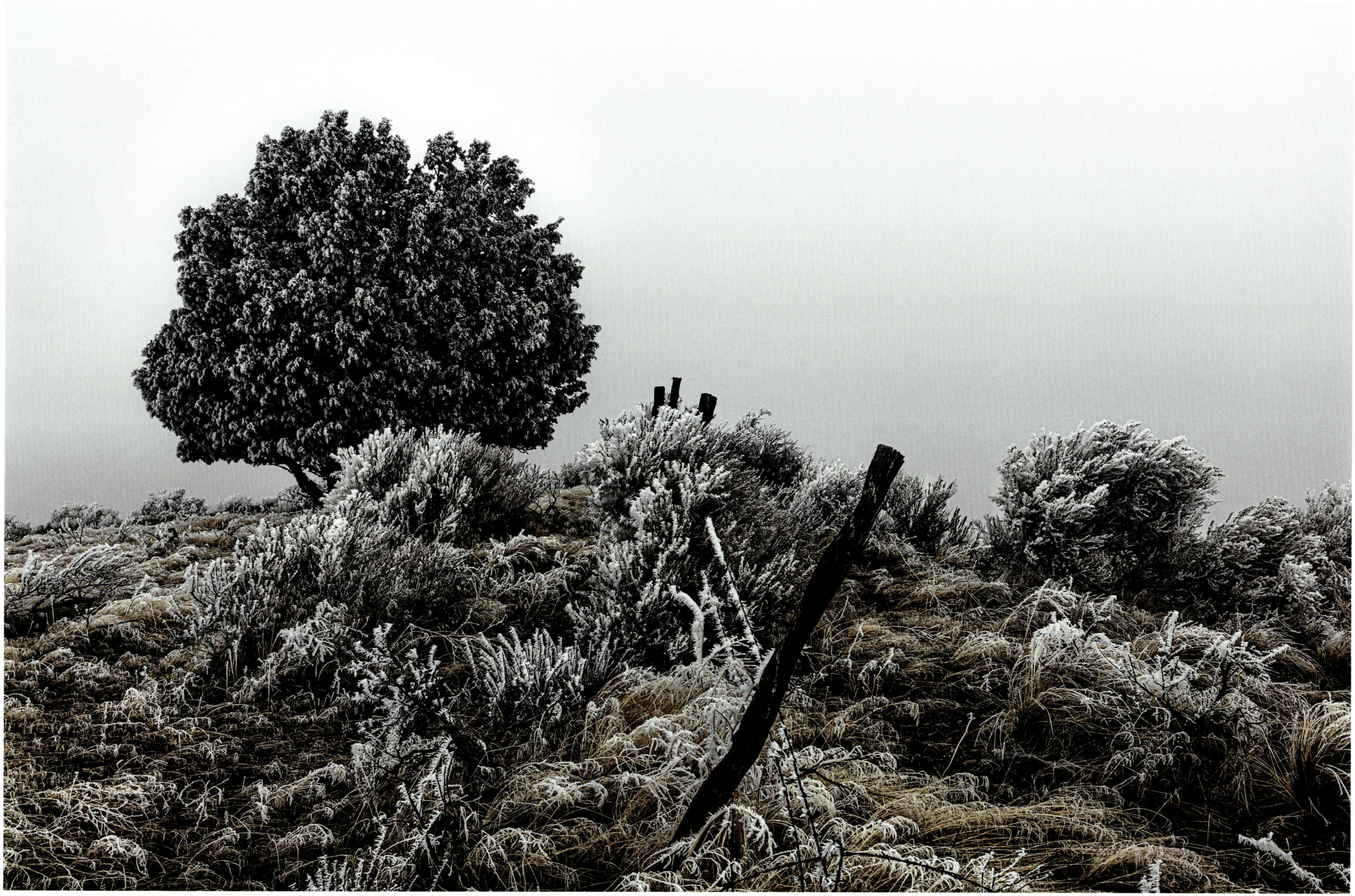

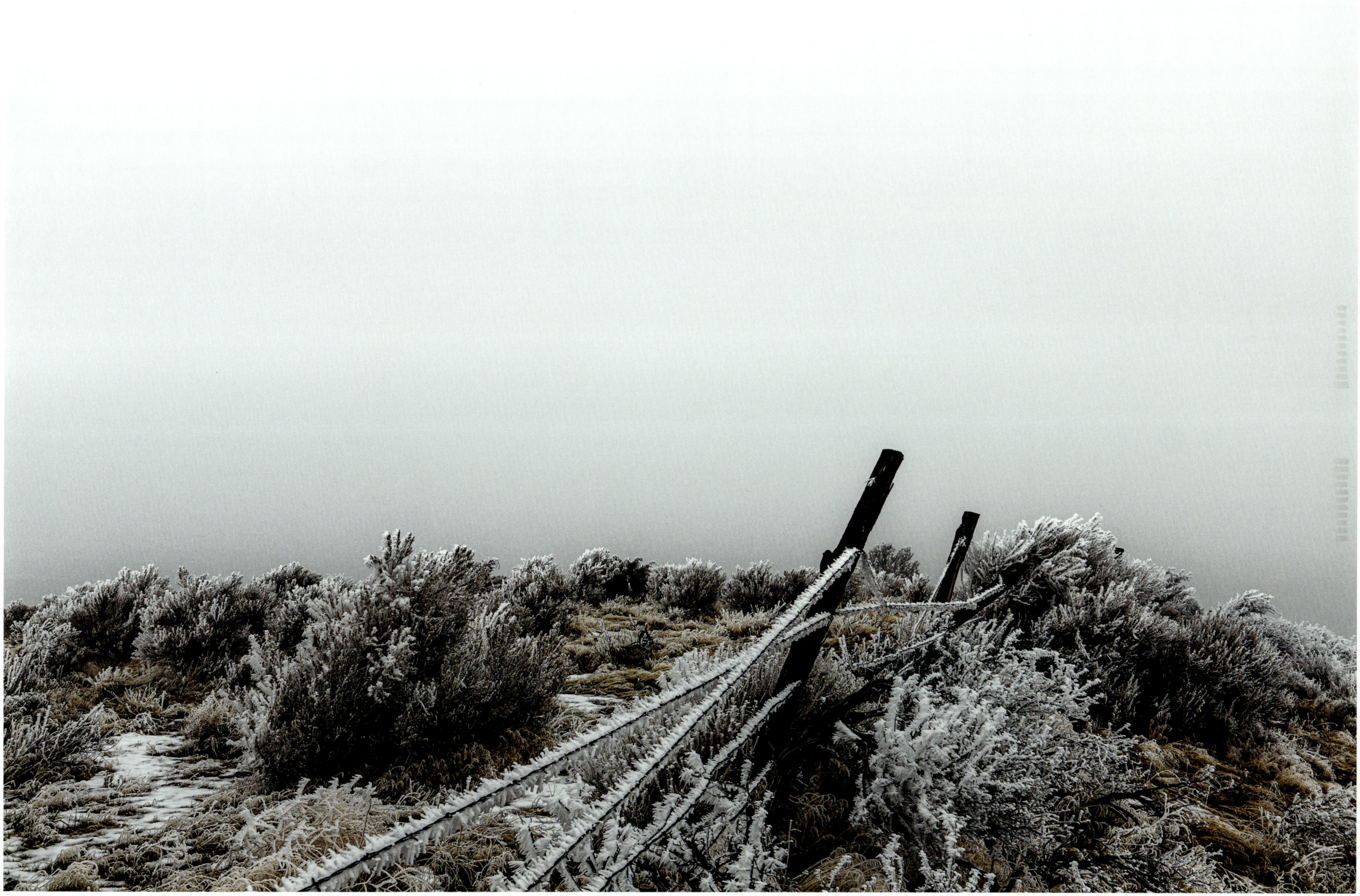

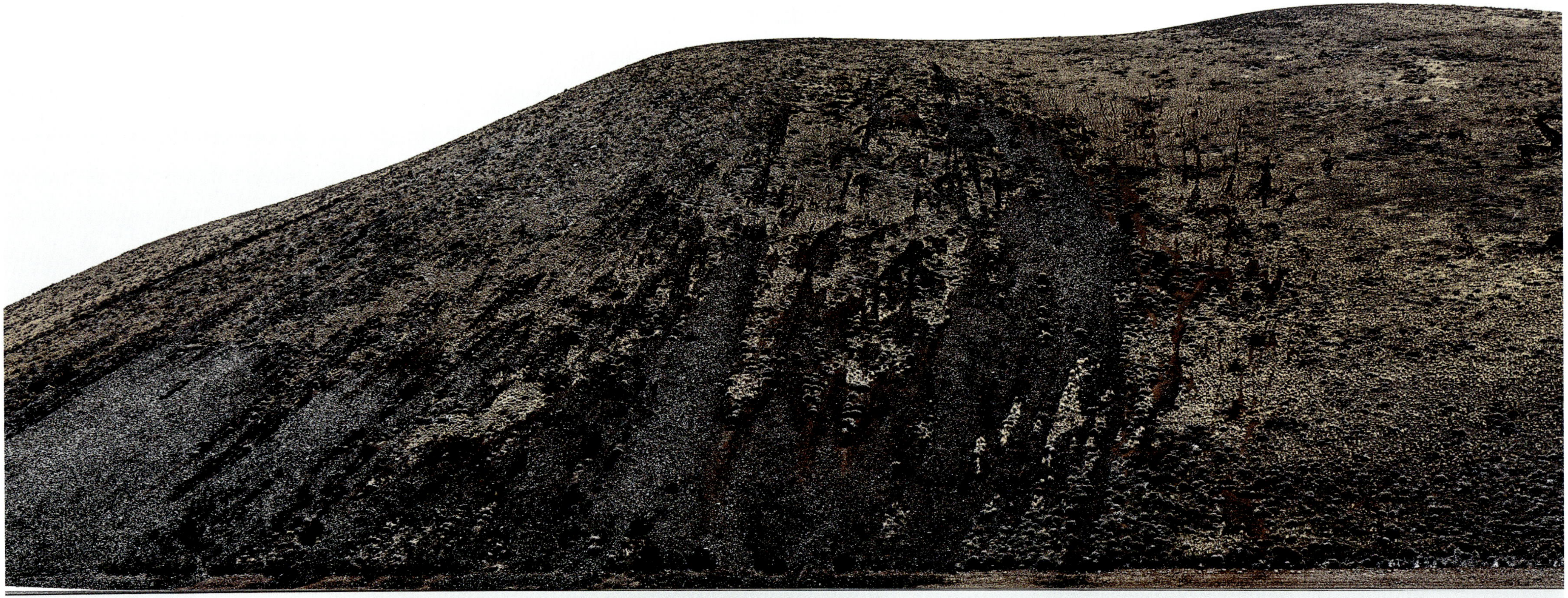

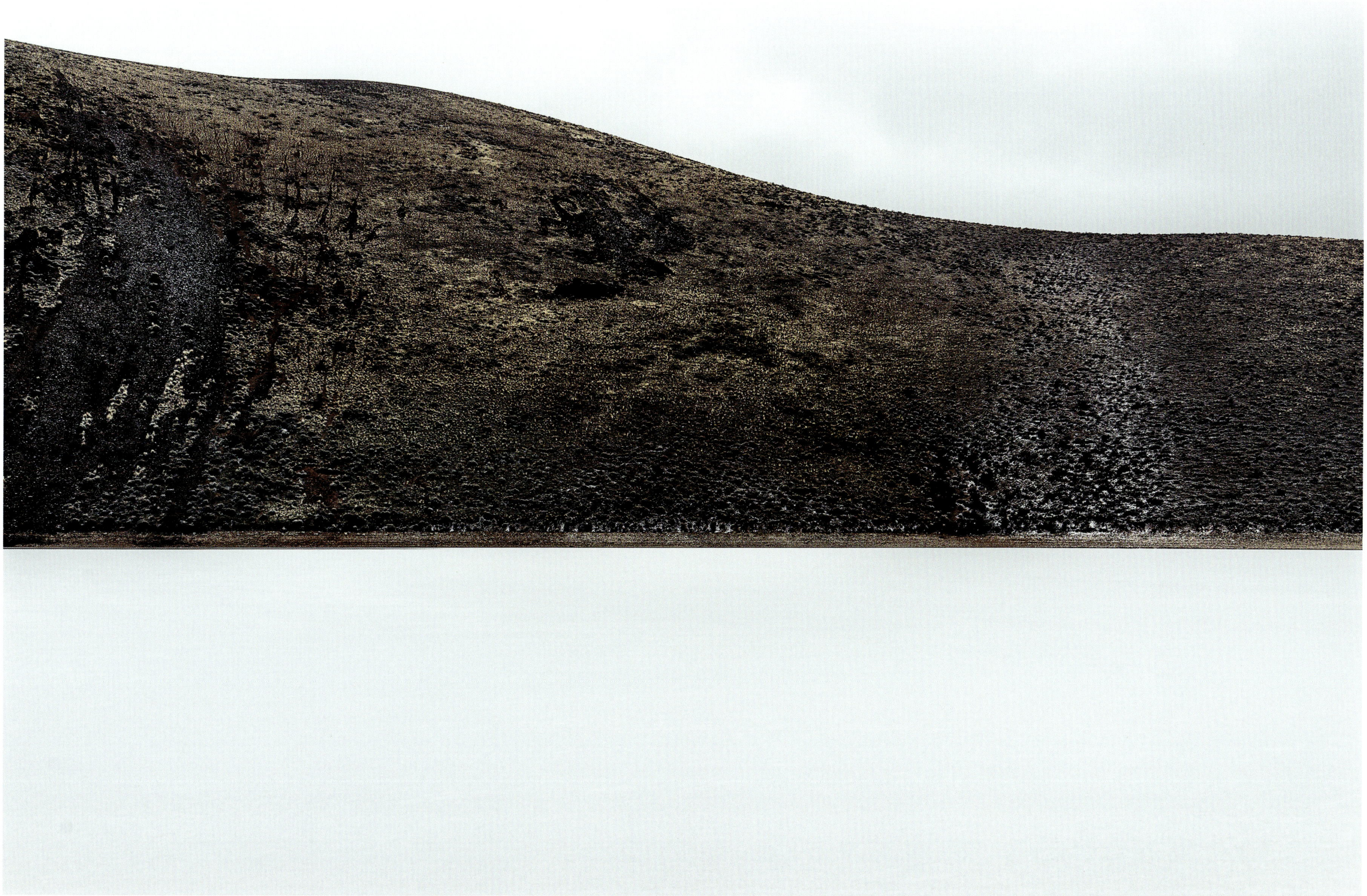

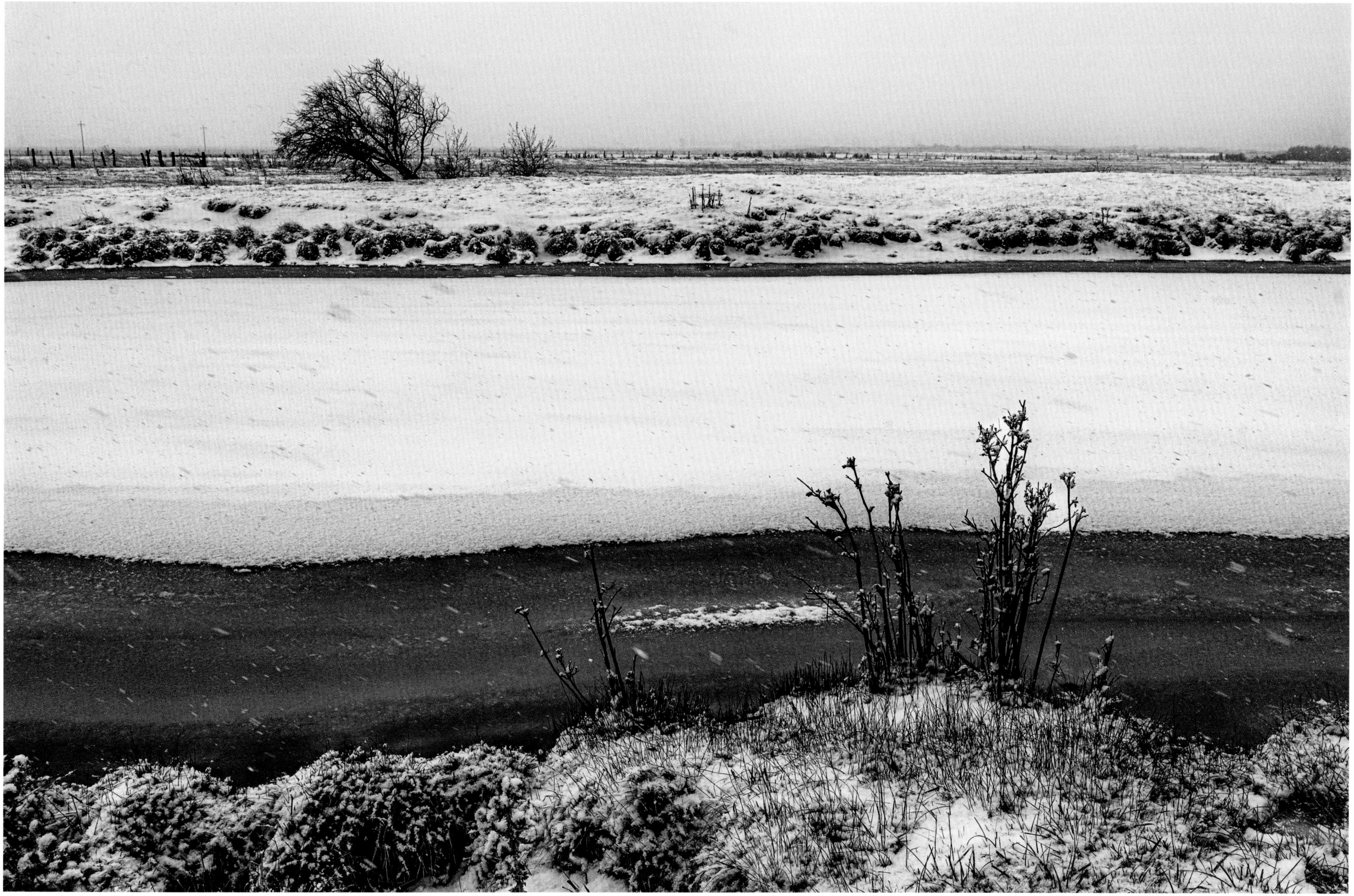

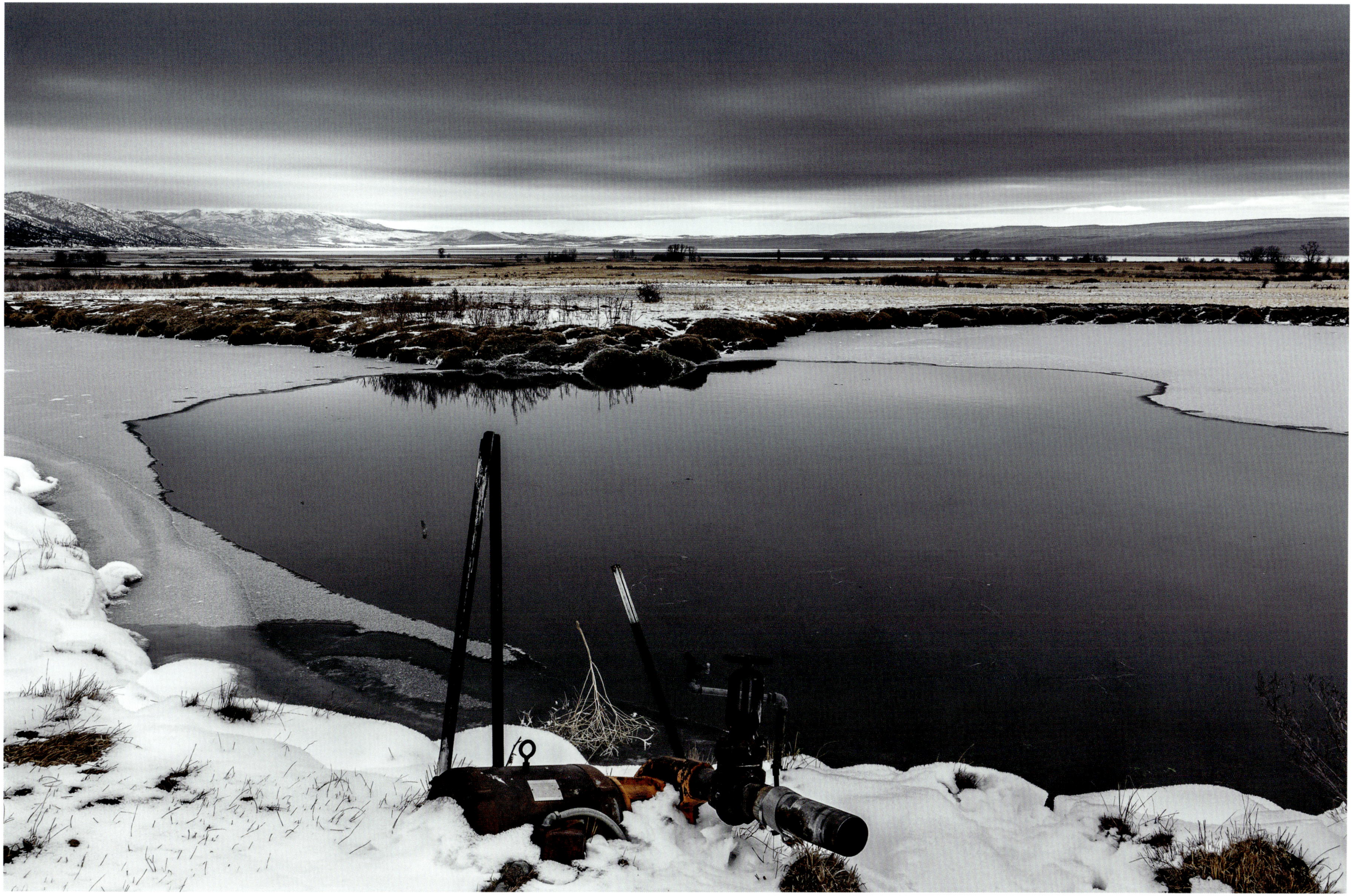

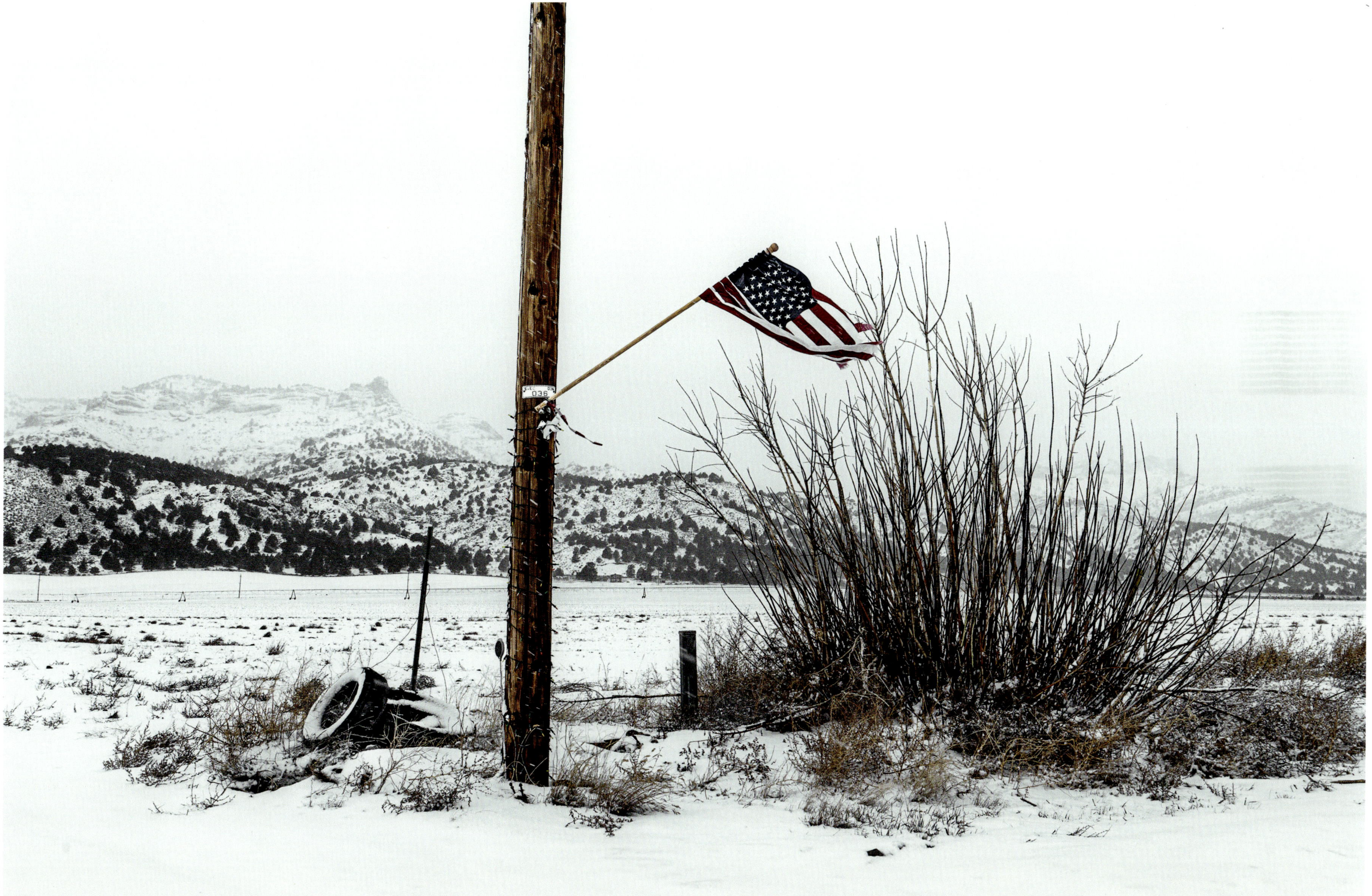
036

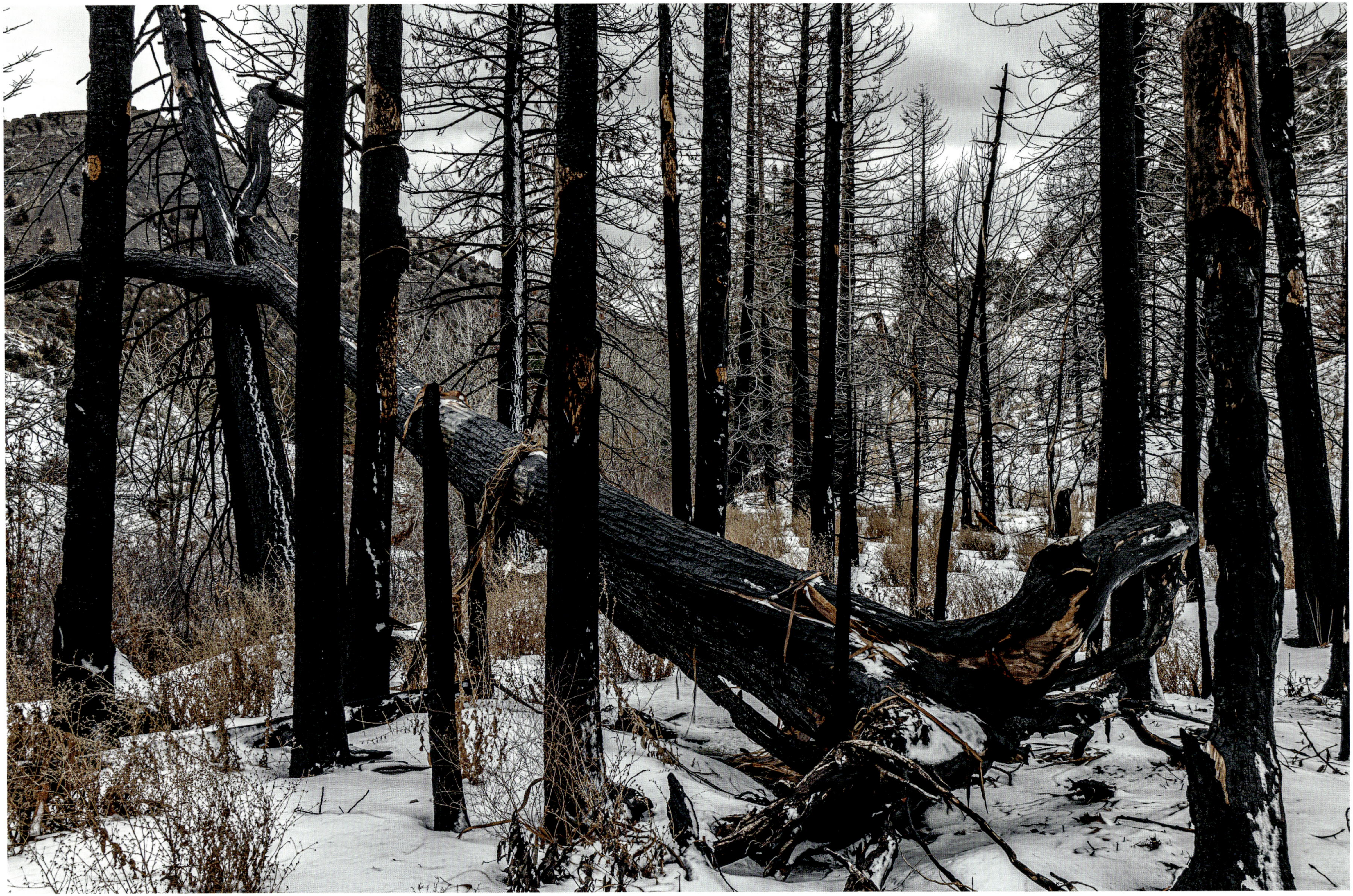

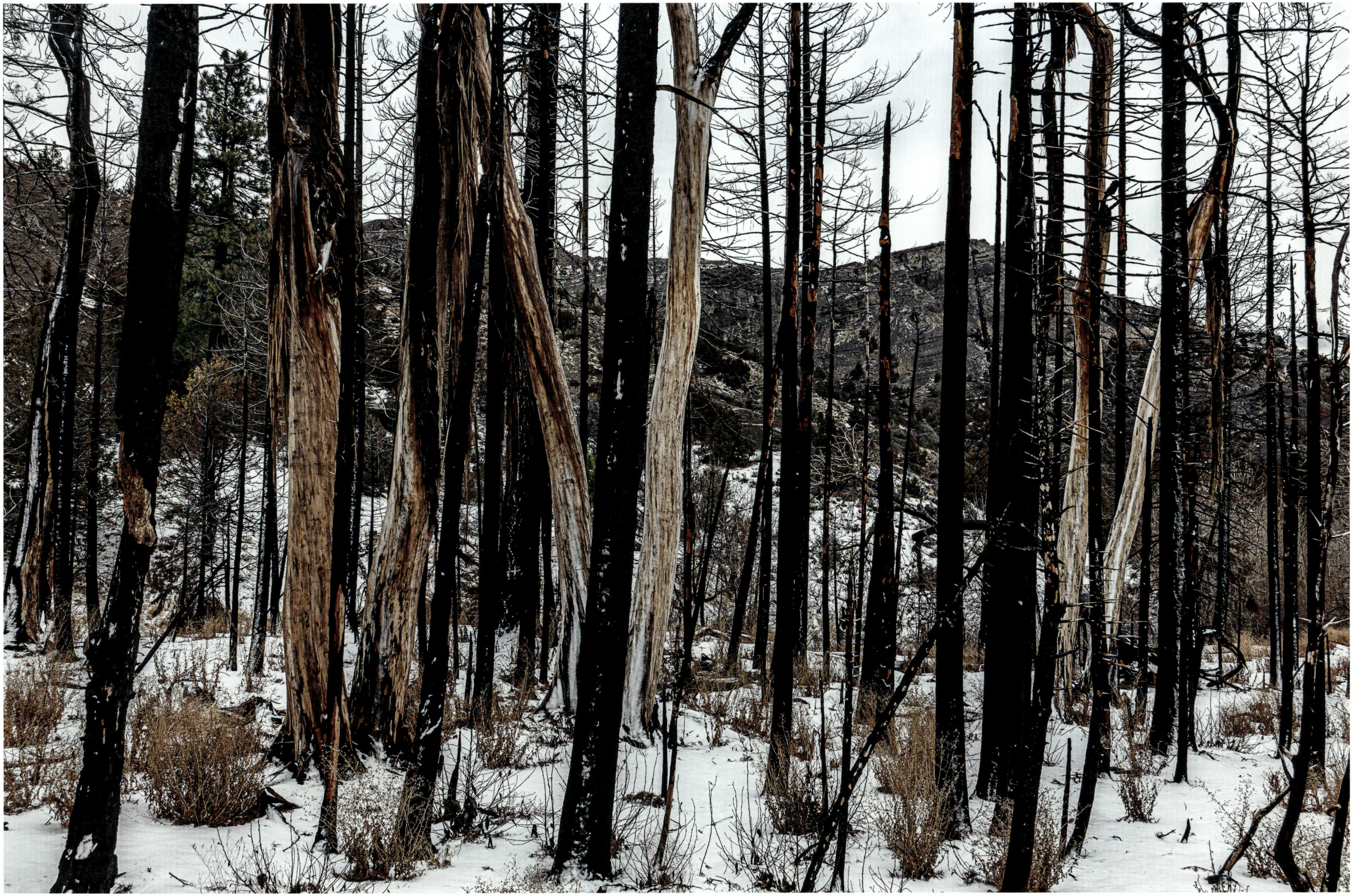

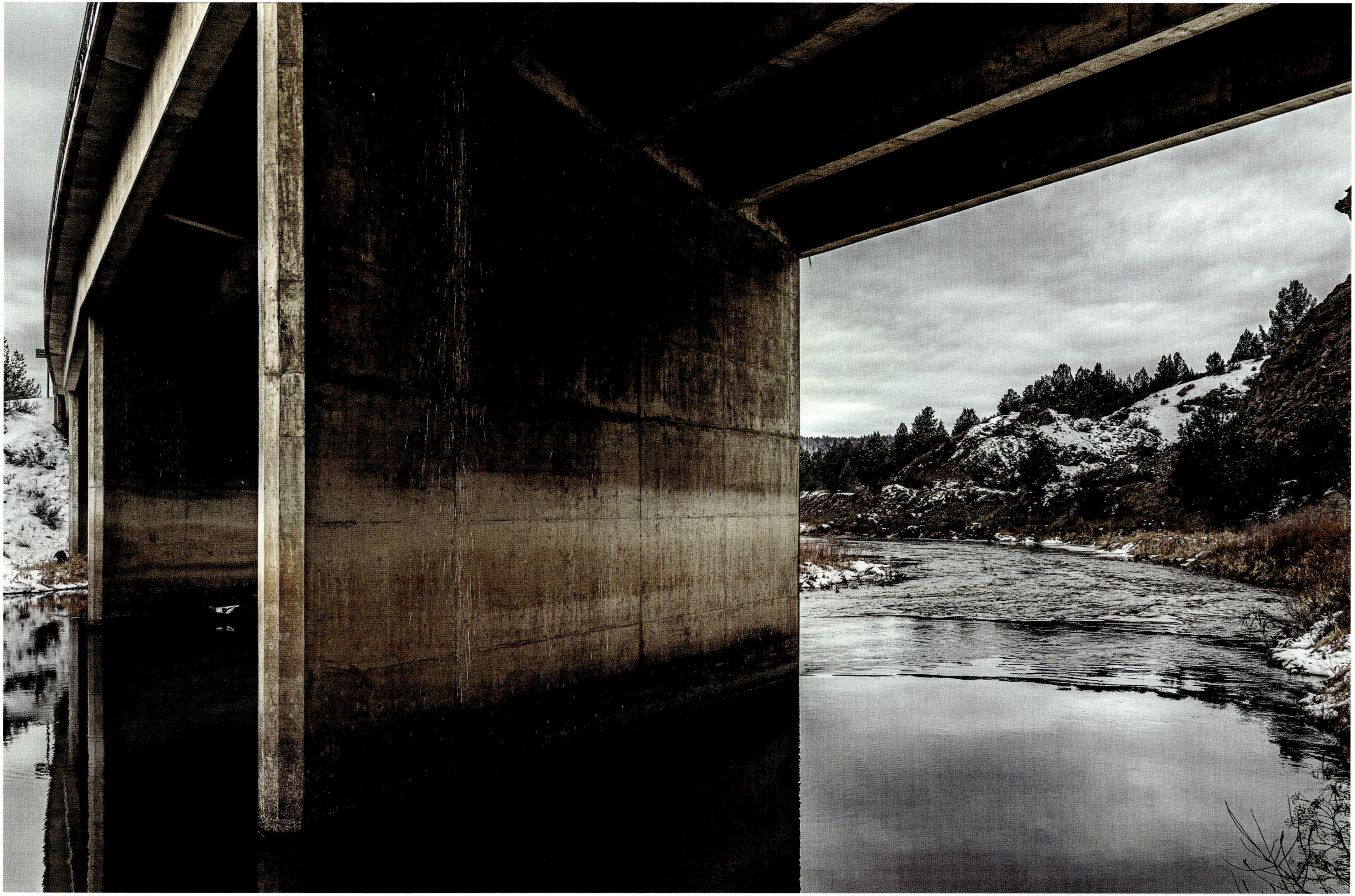

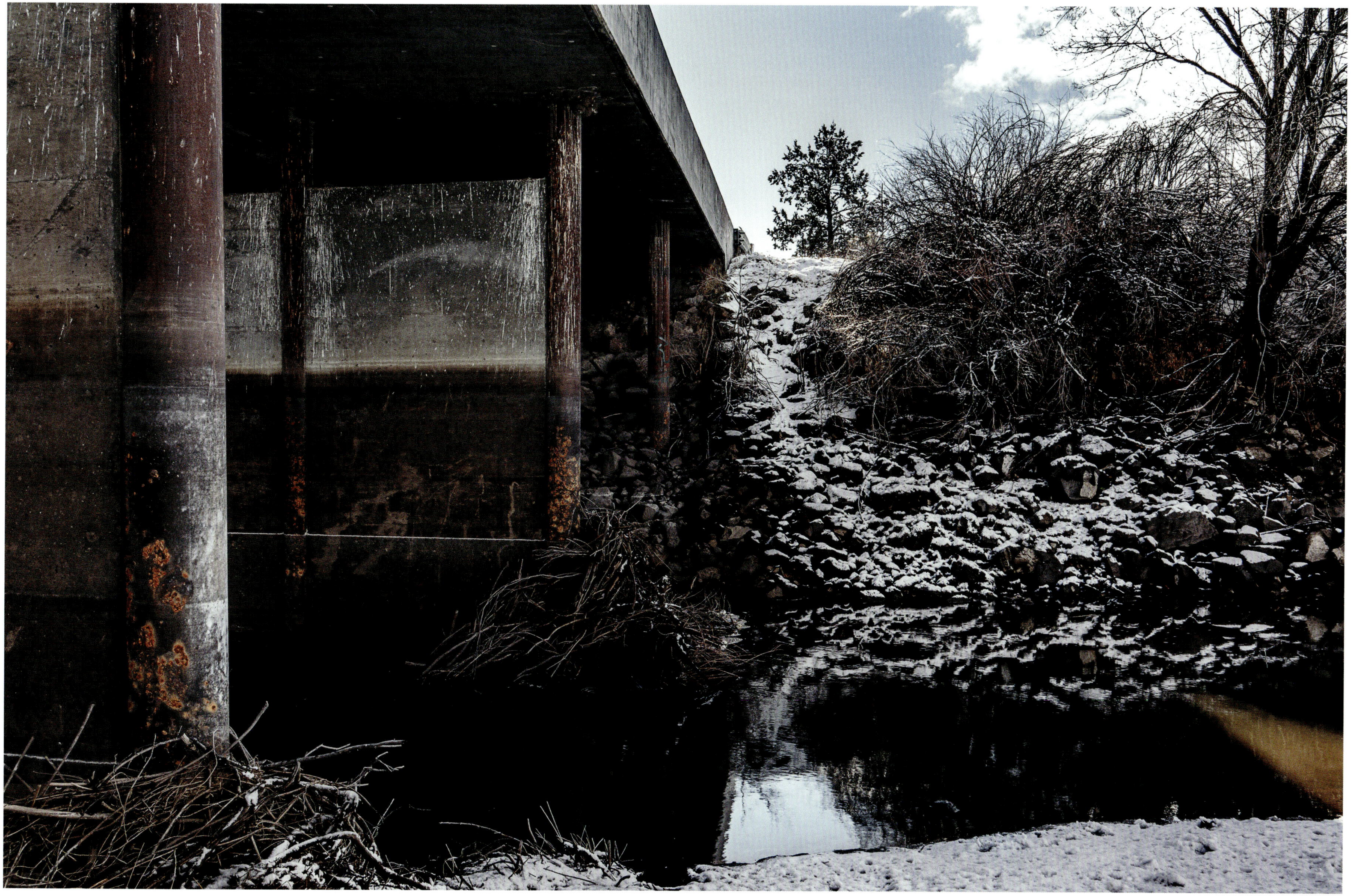

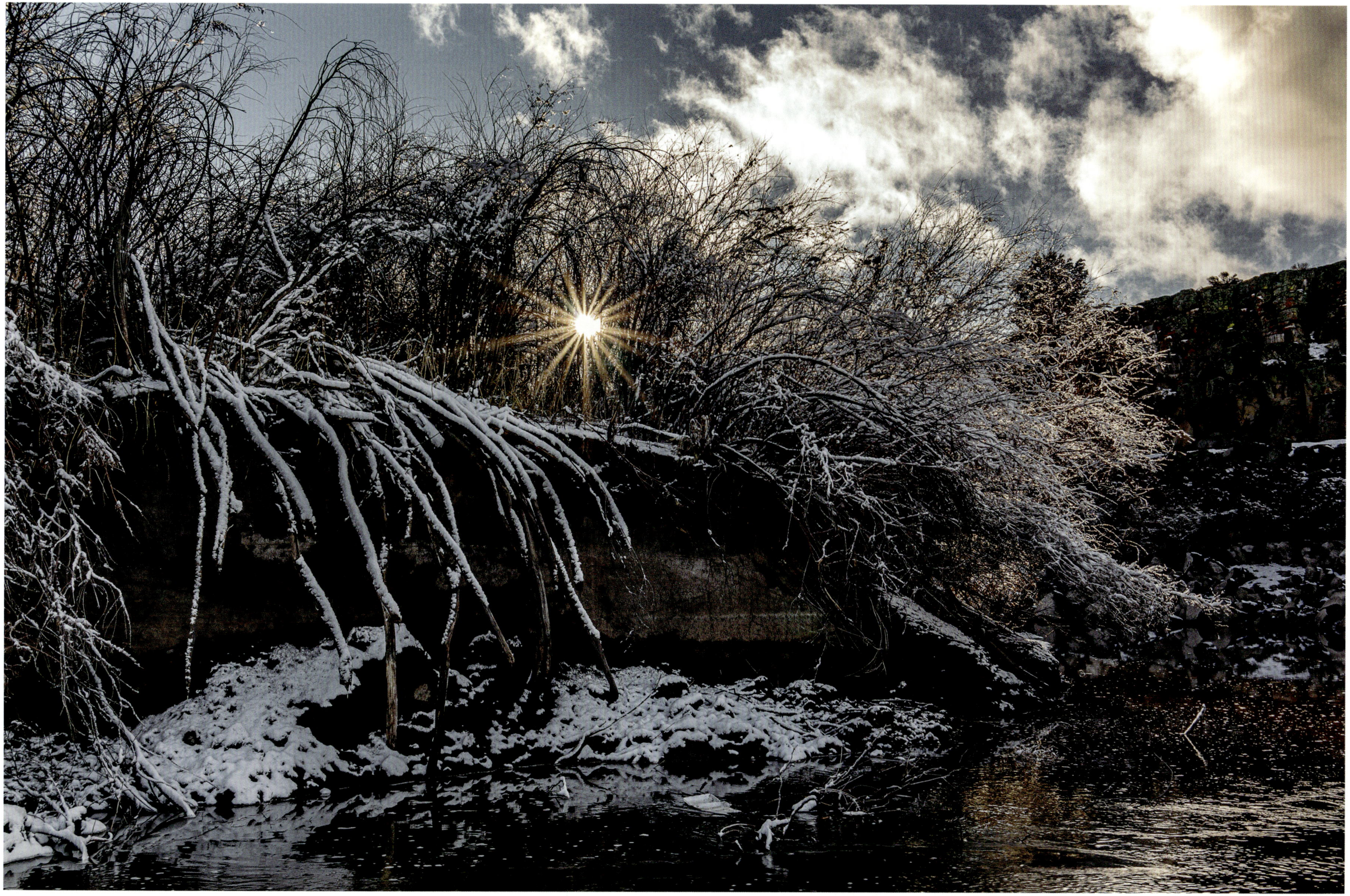

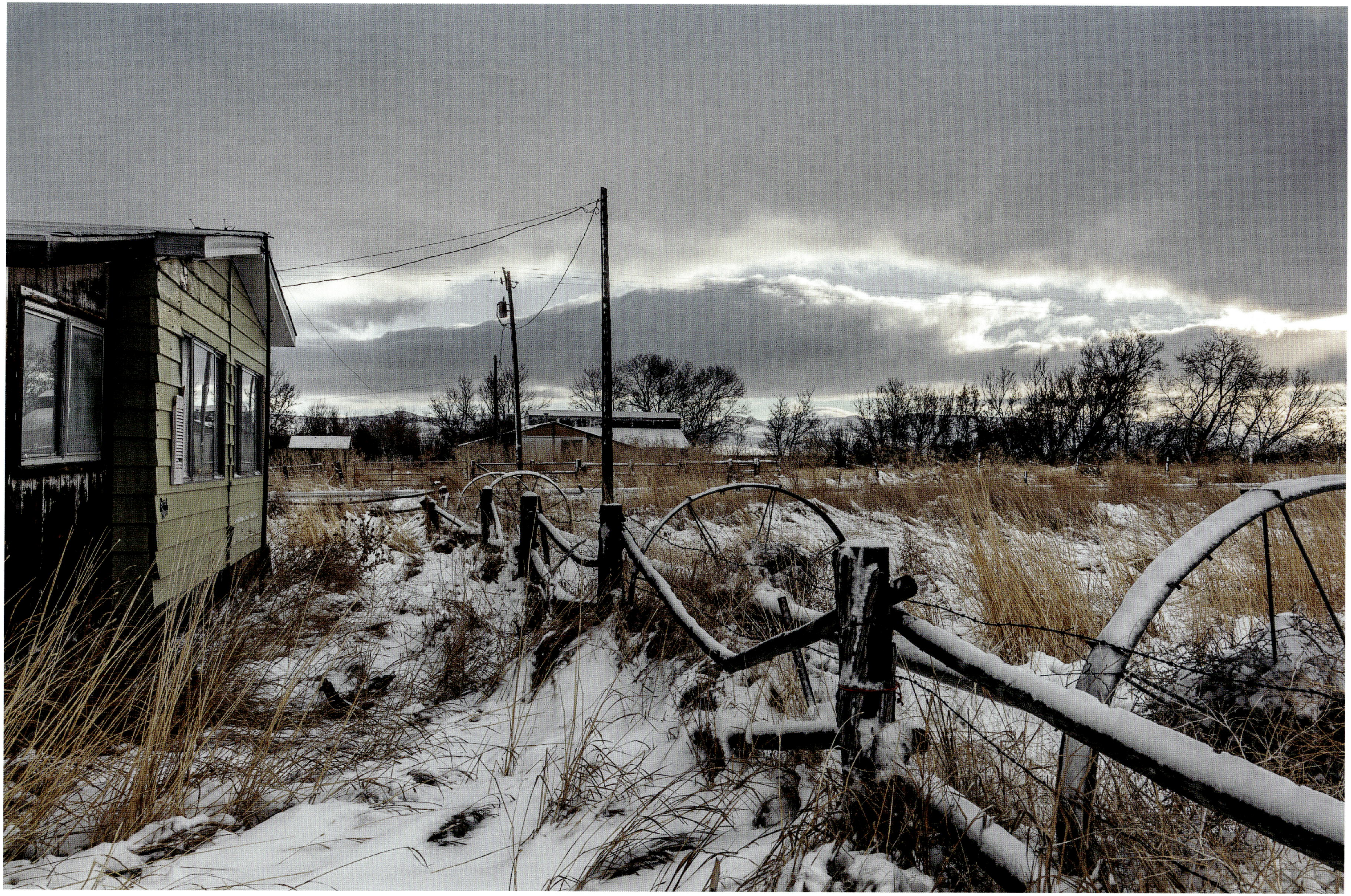

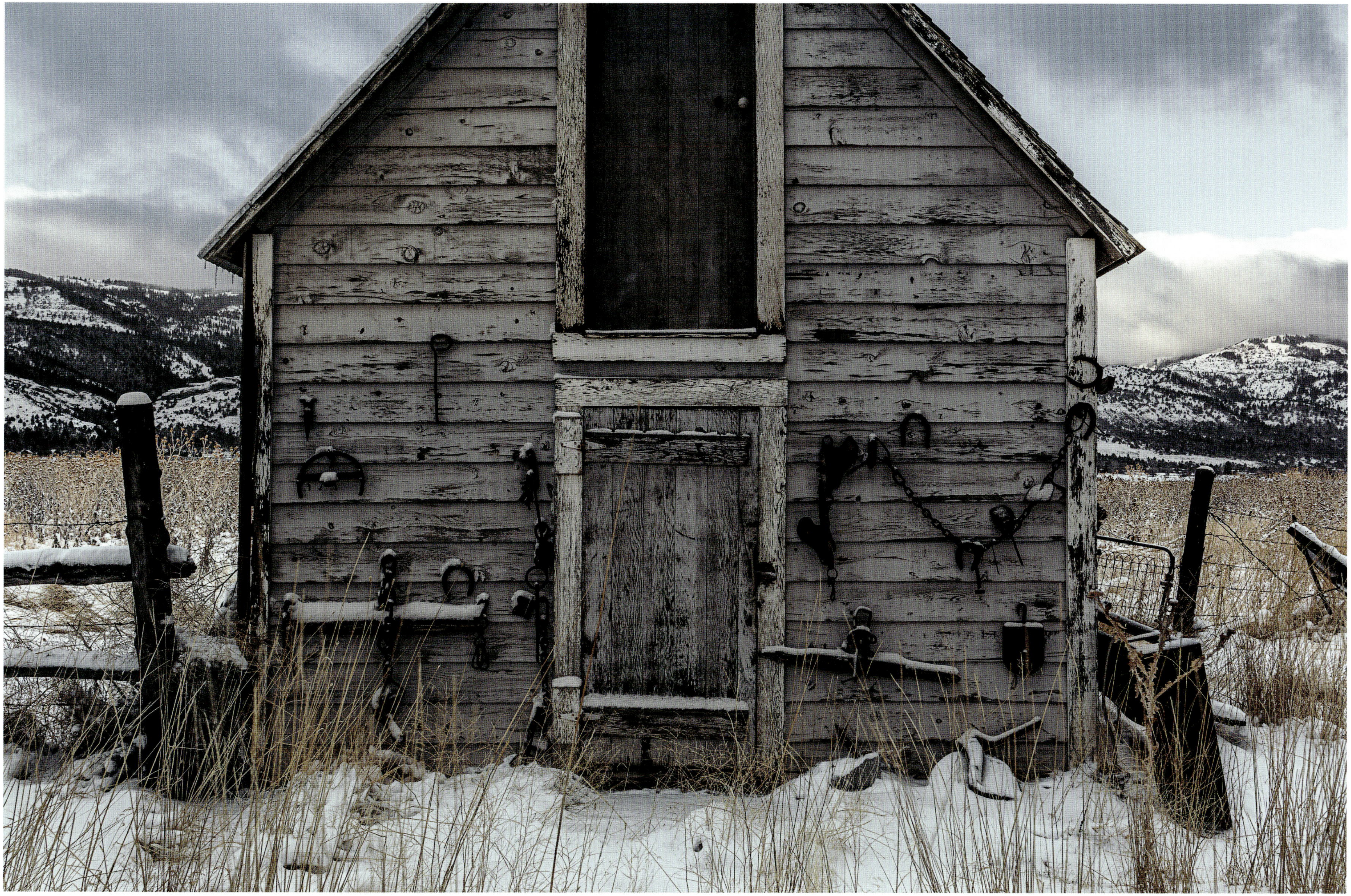

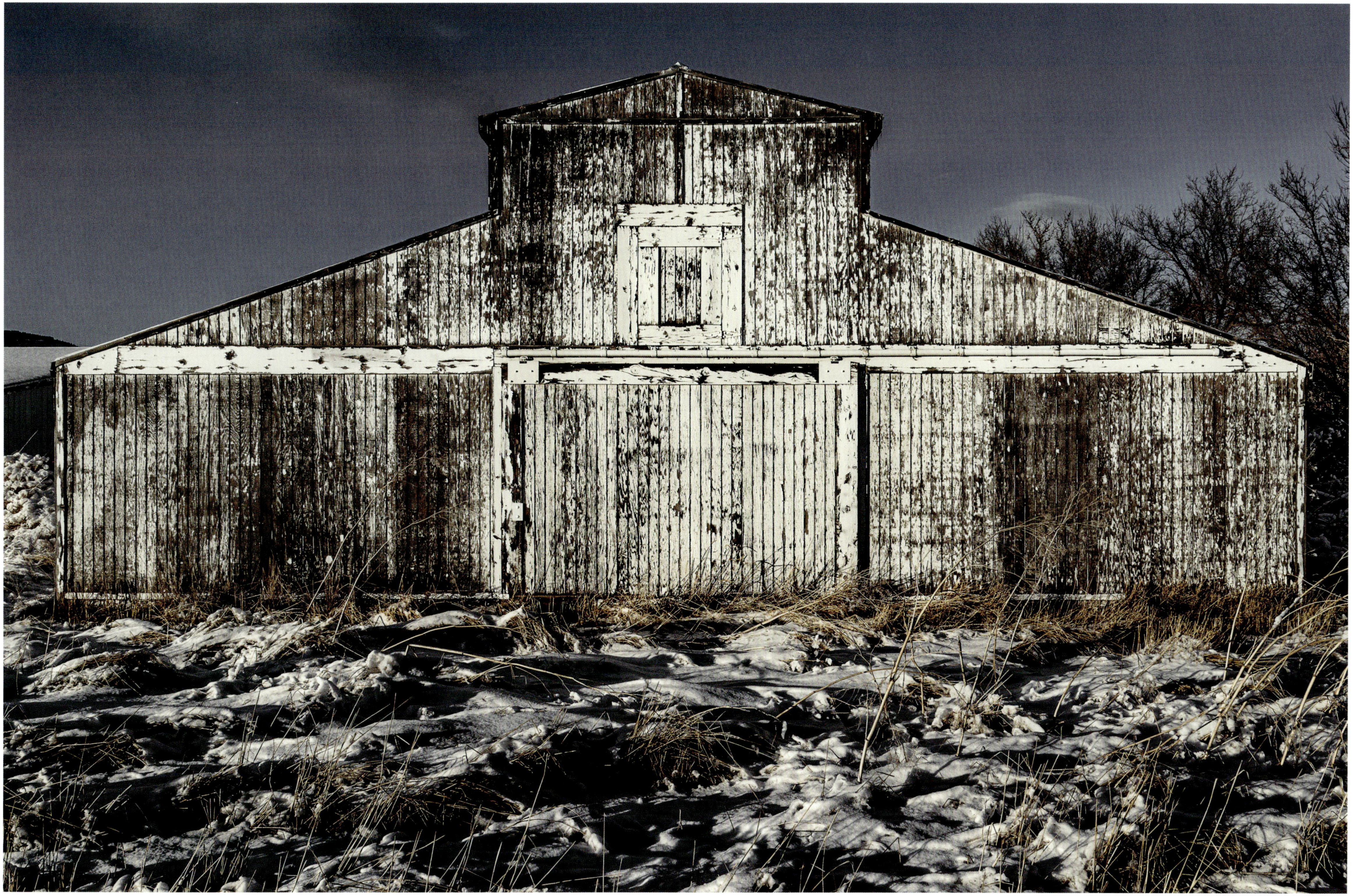

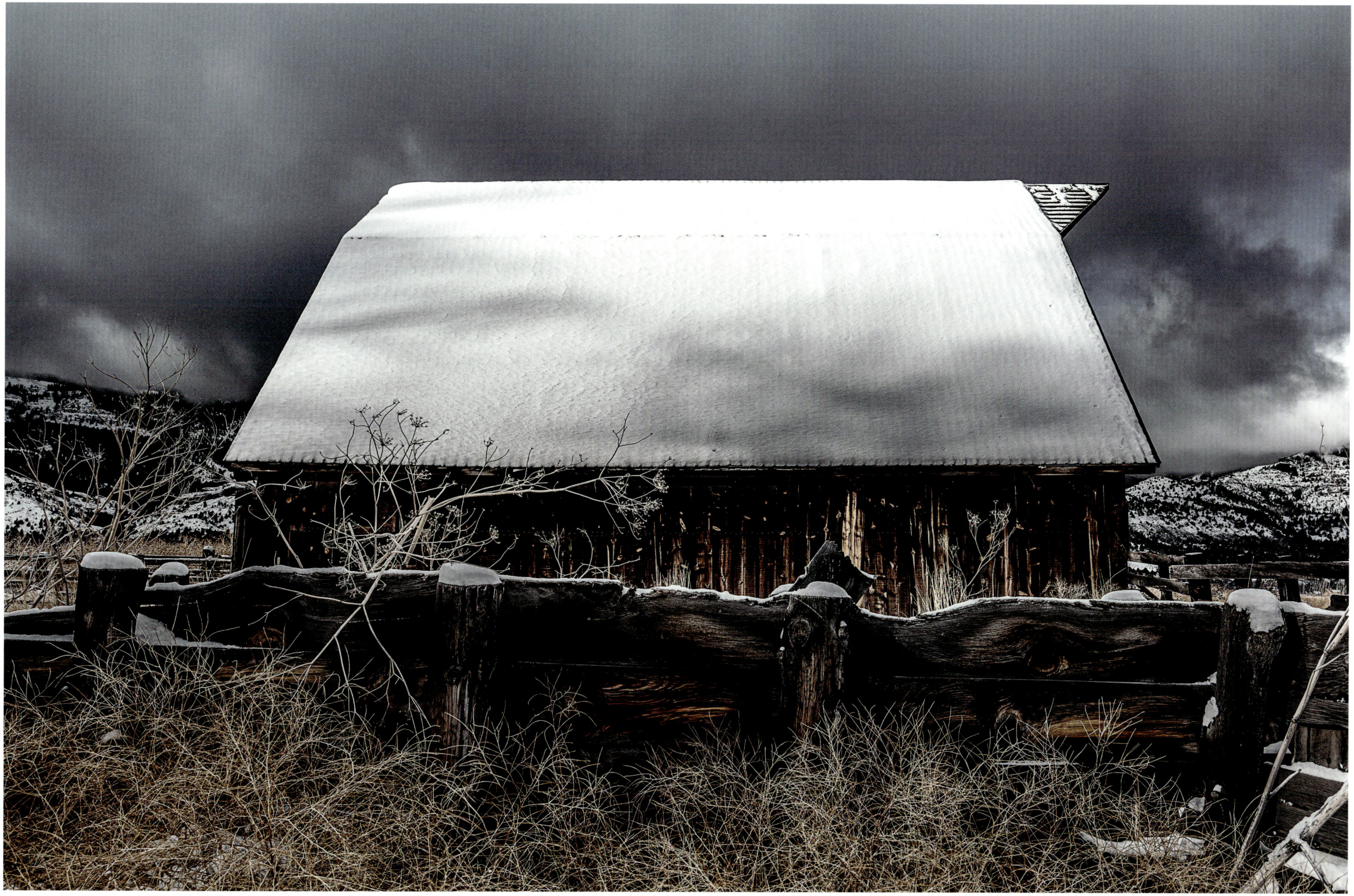

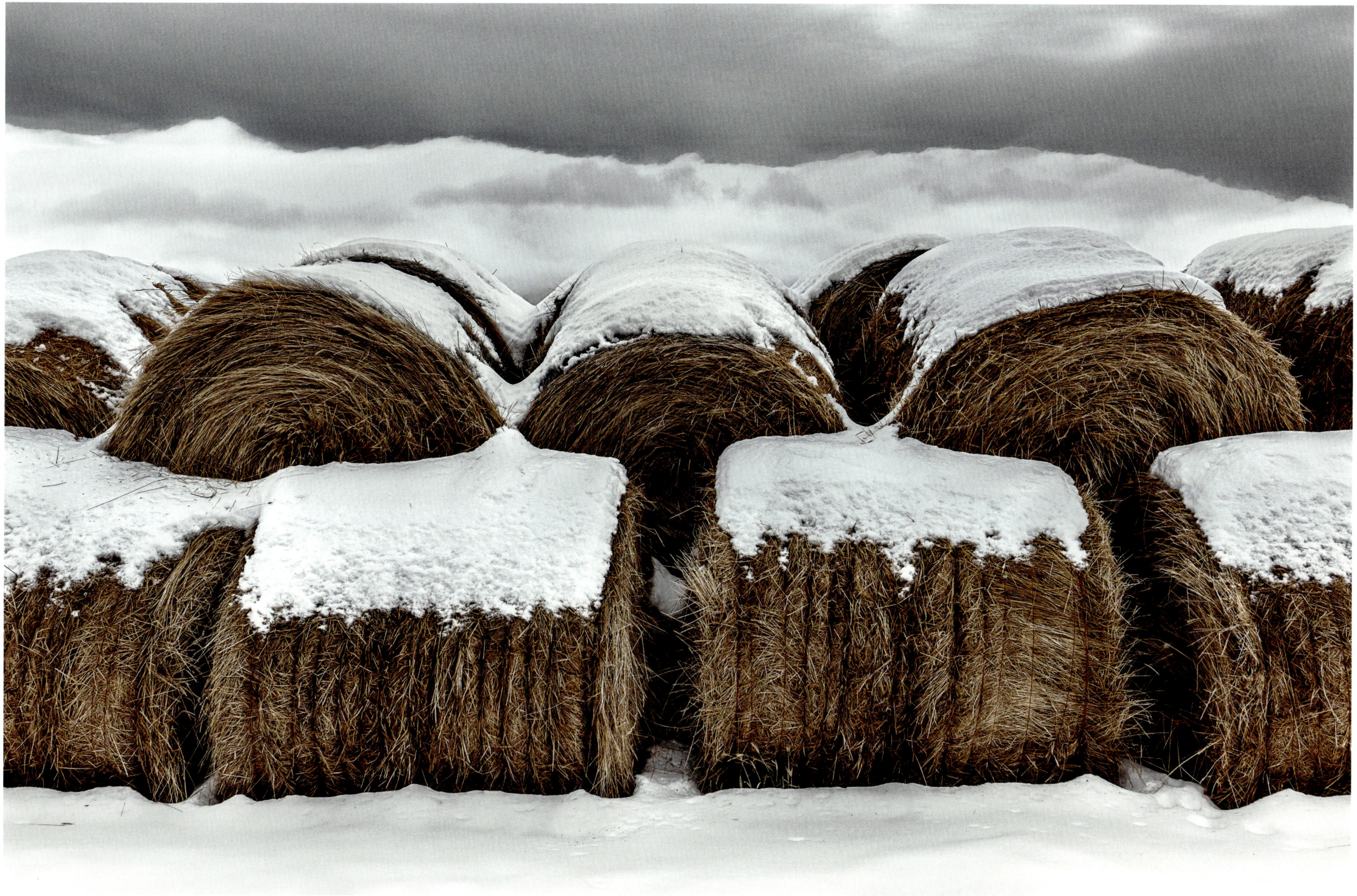

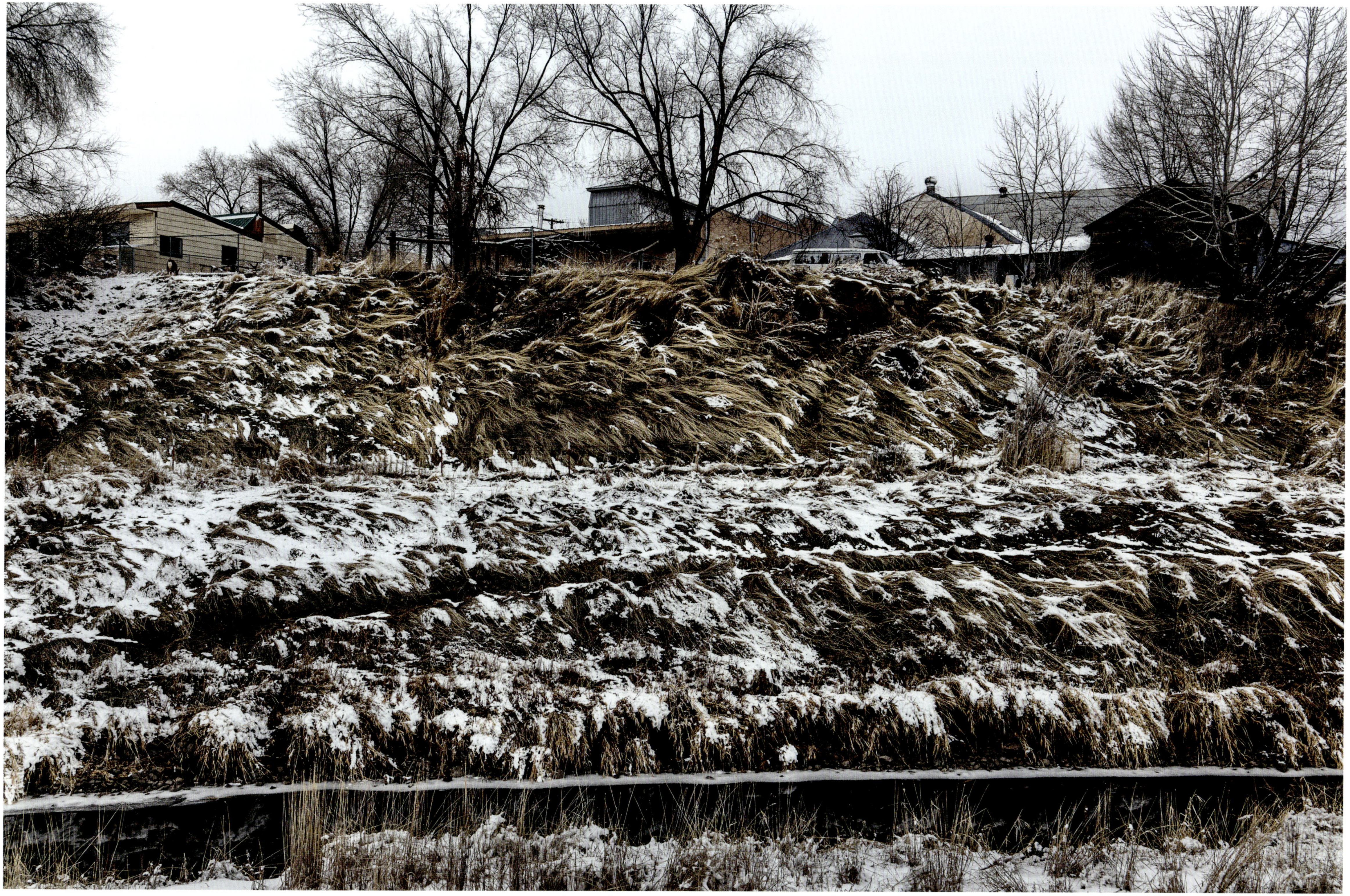

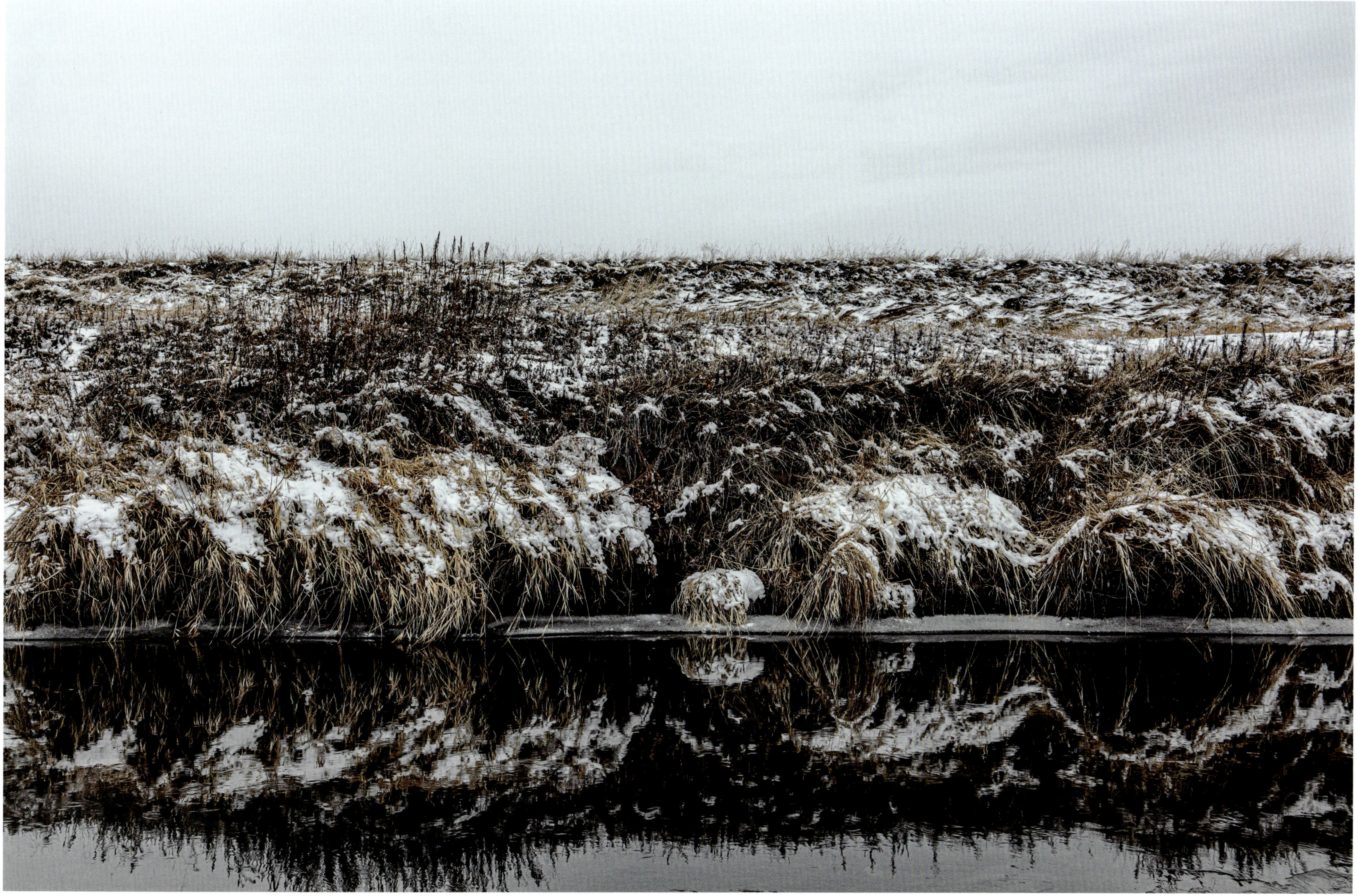

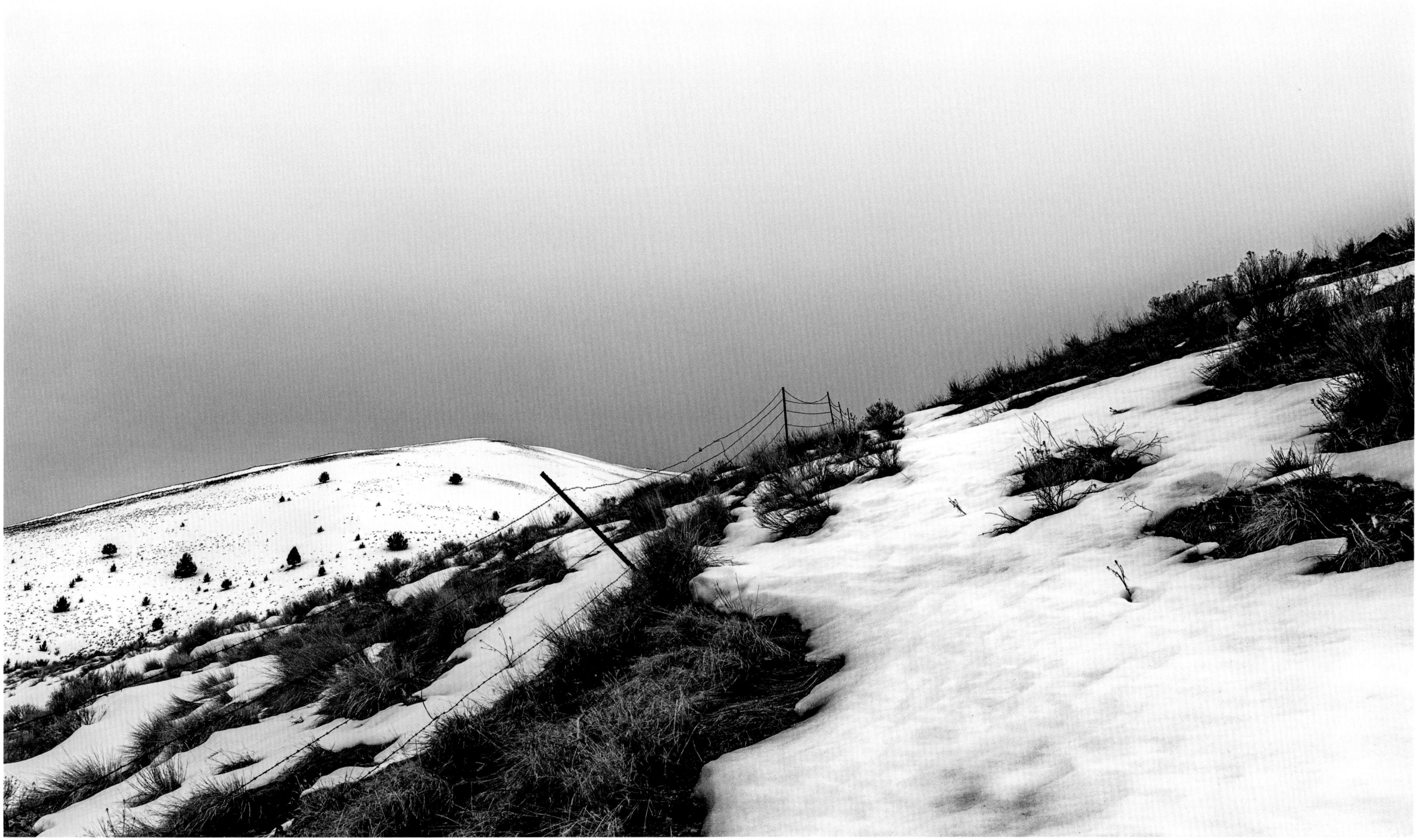

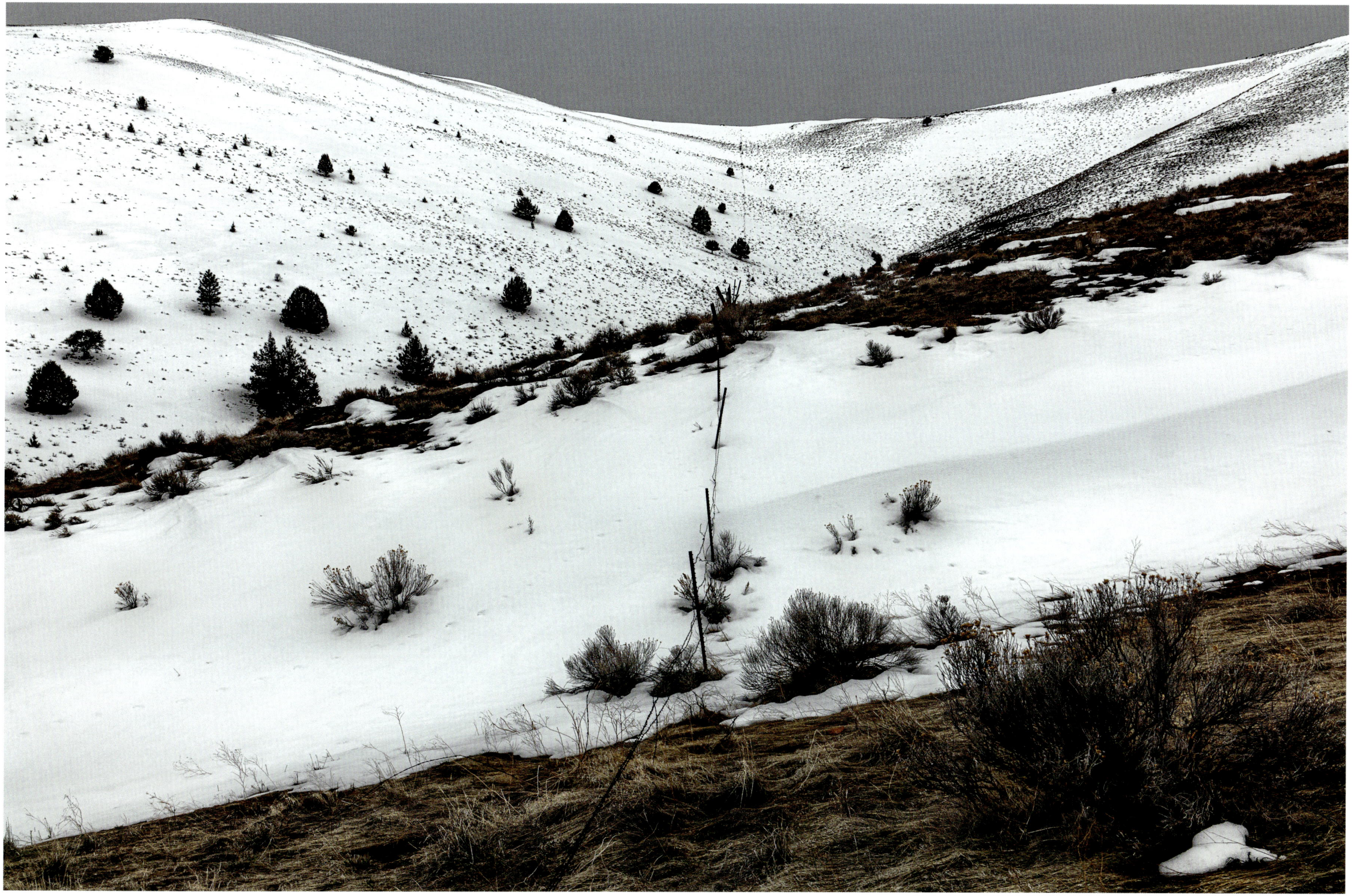

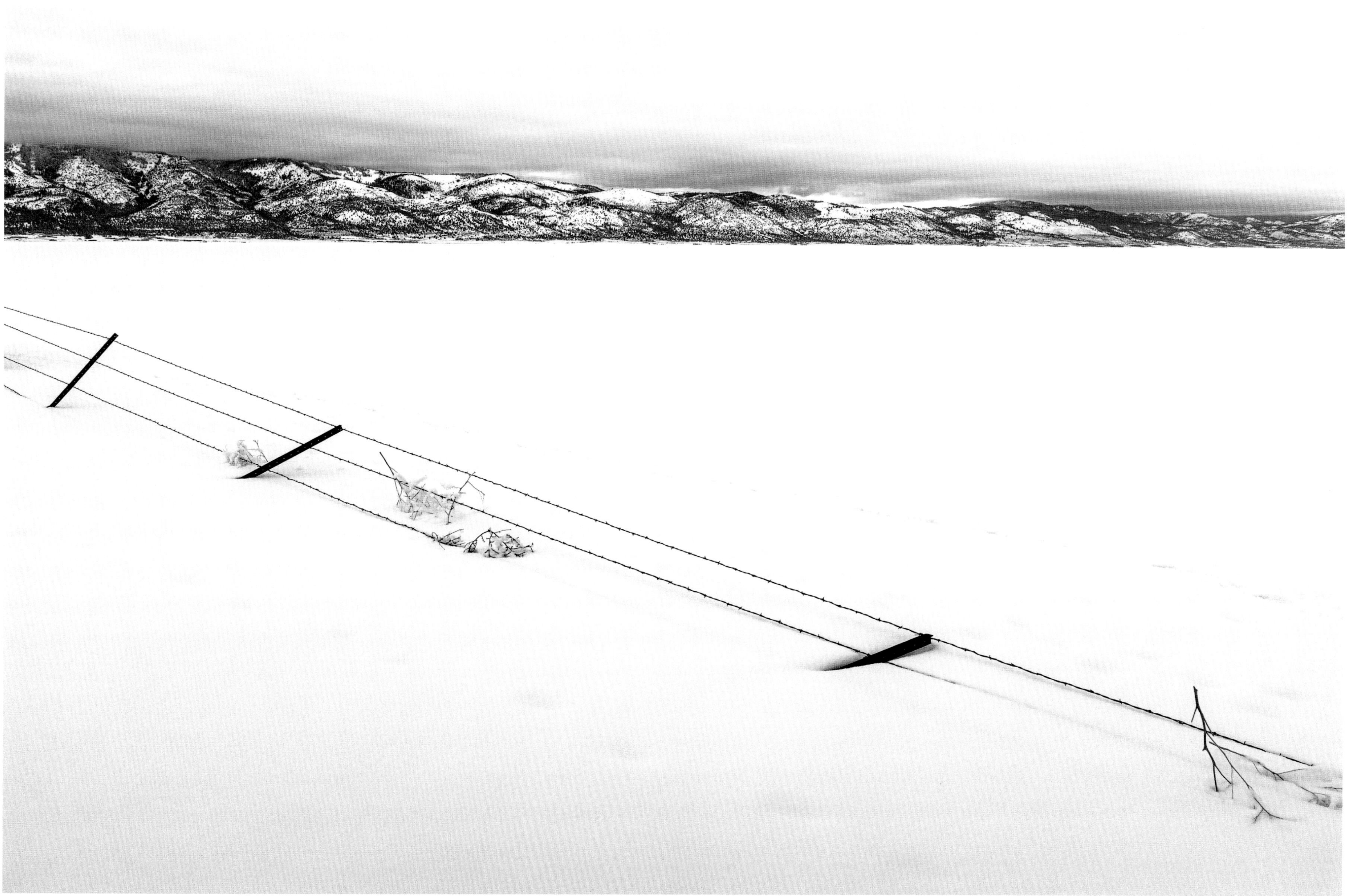

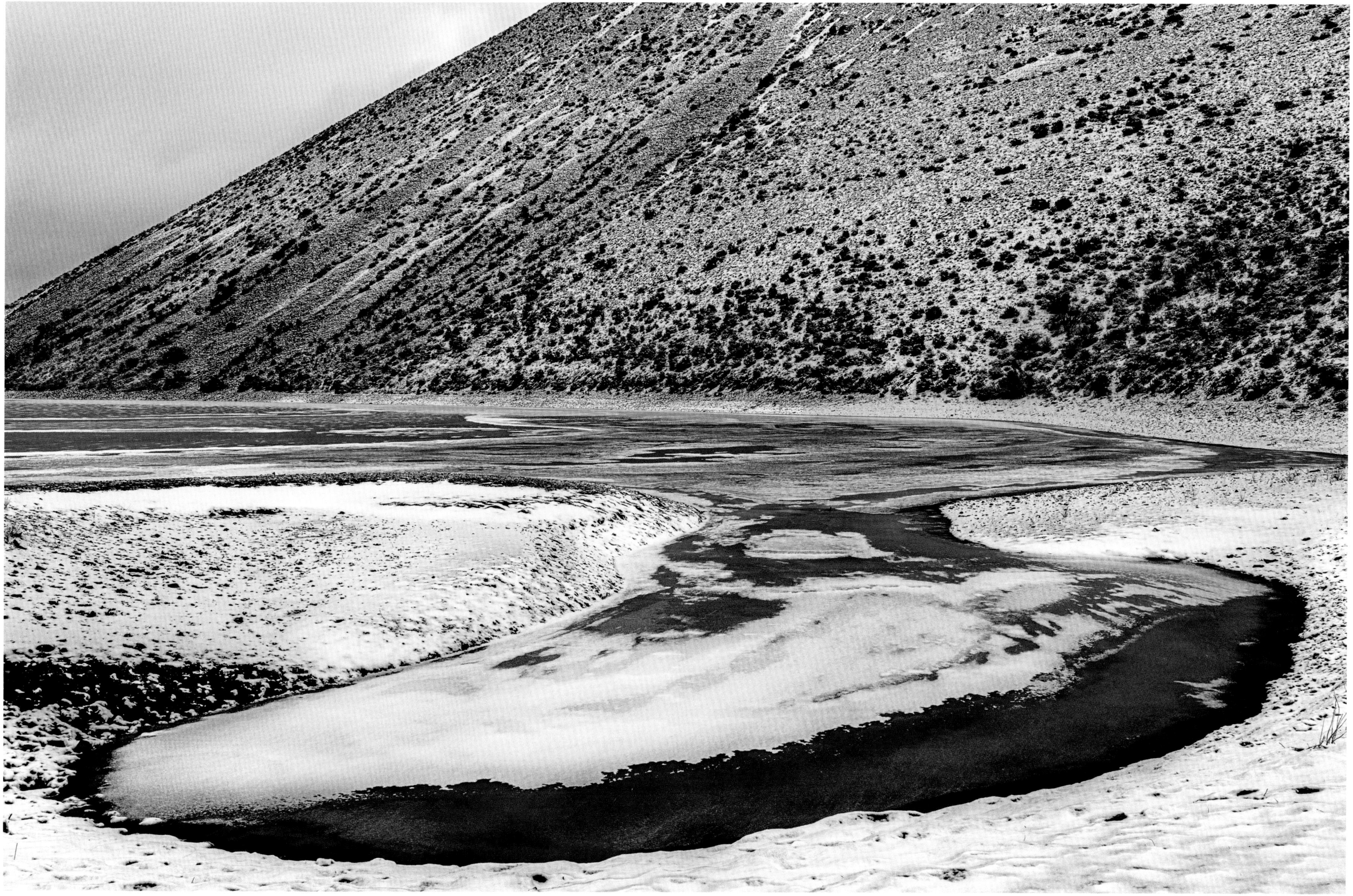

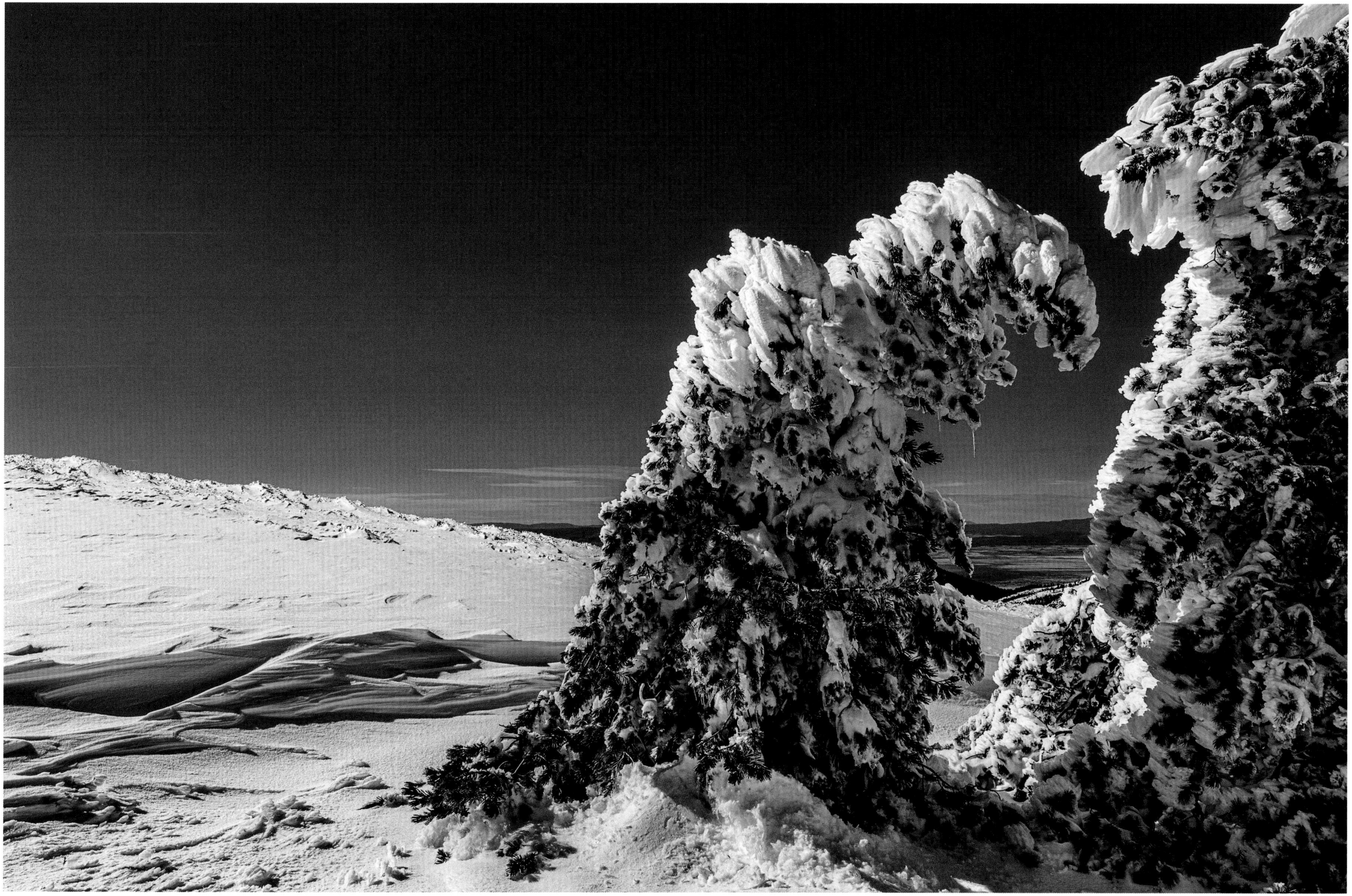

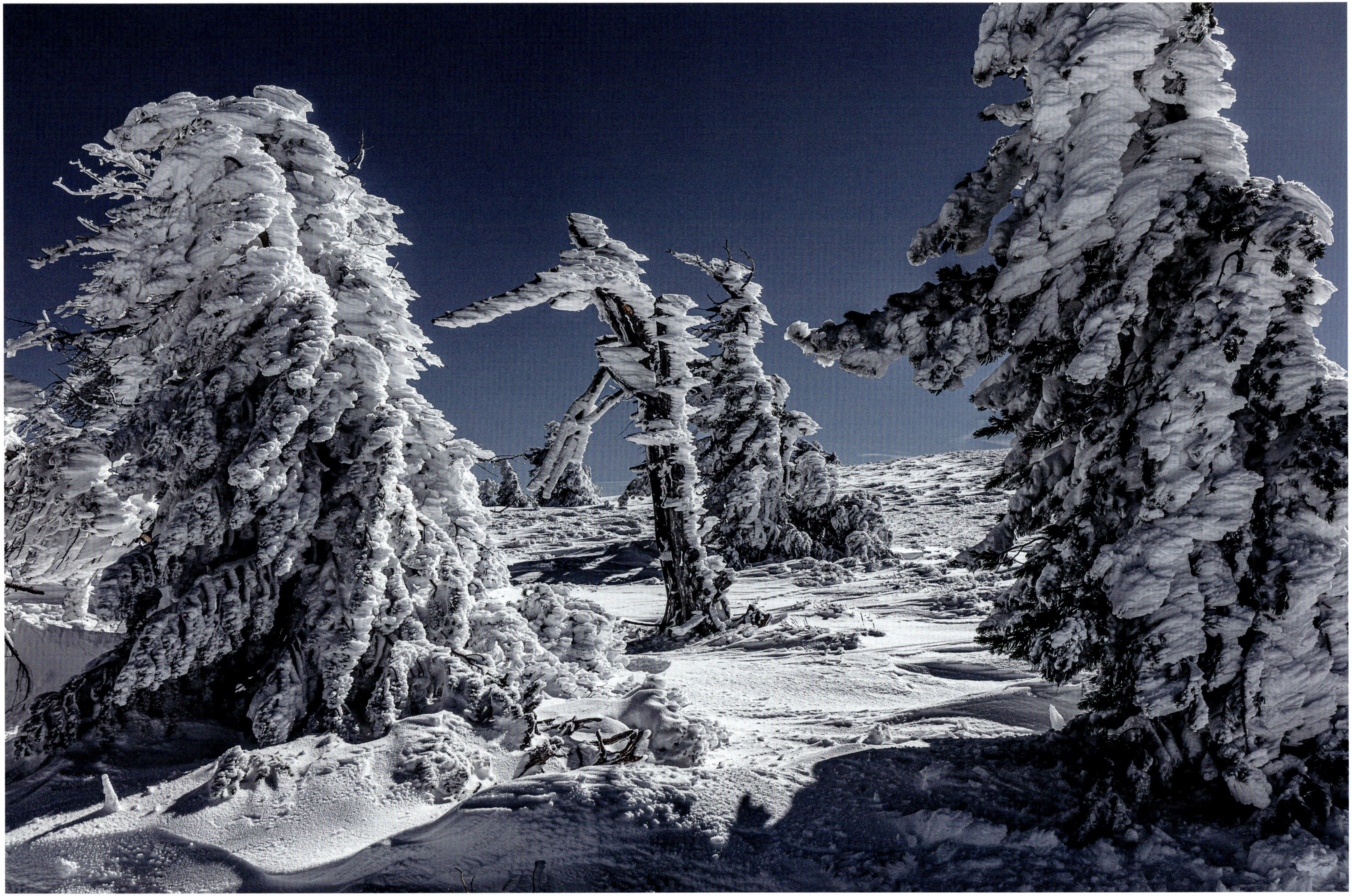

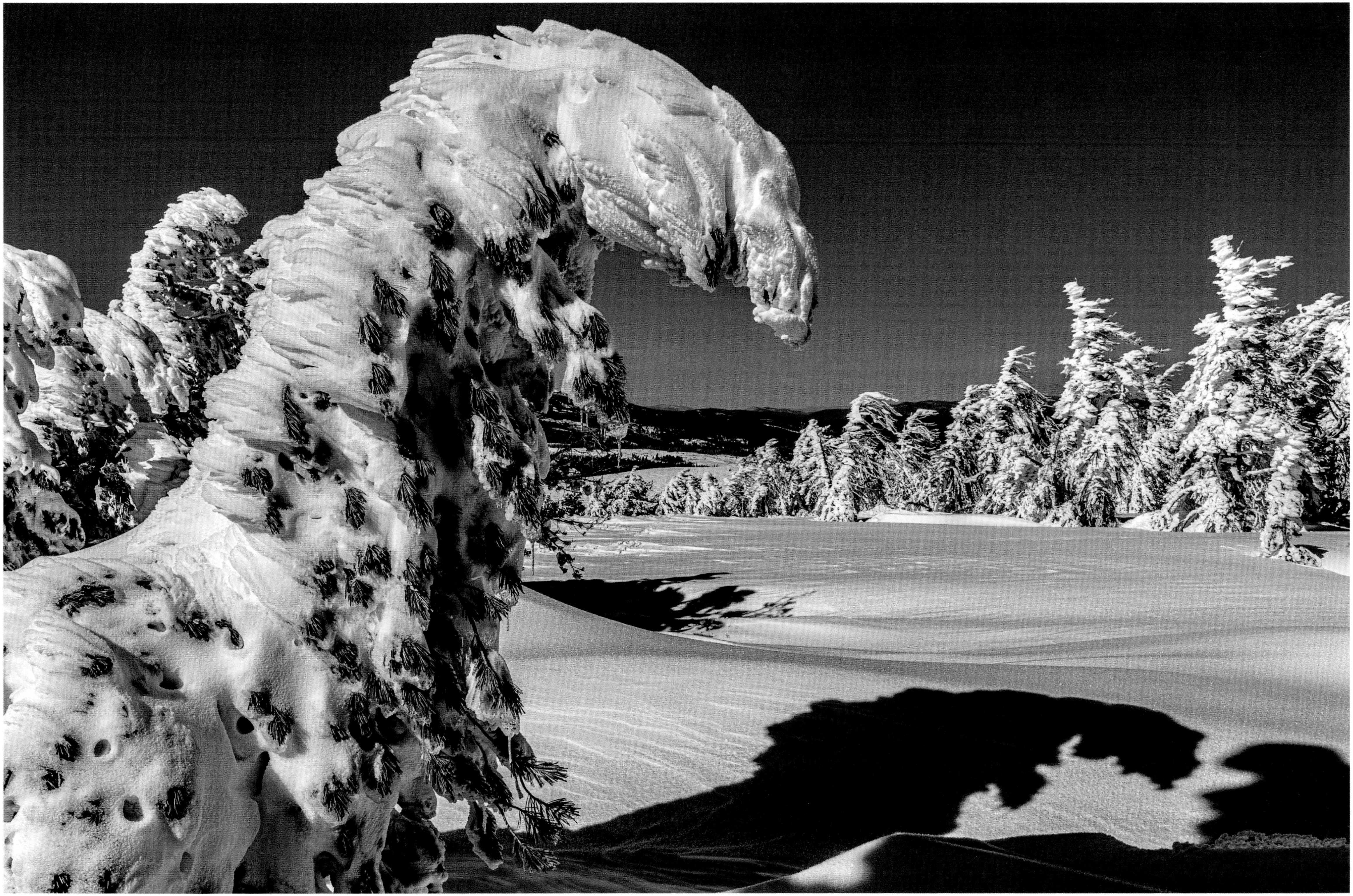

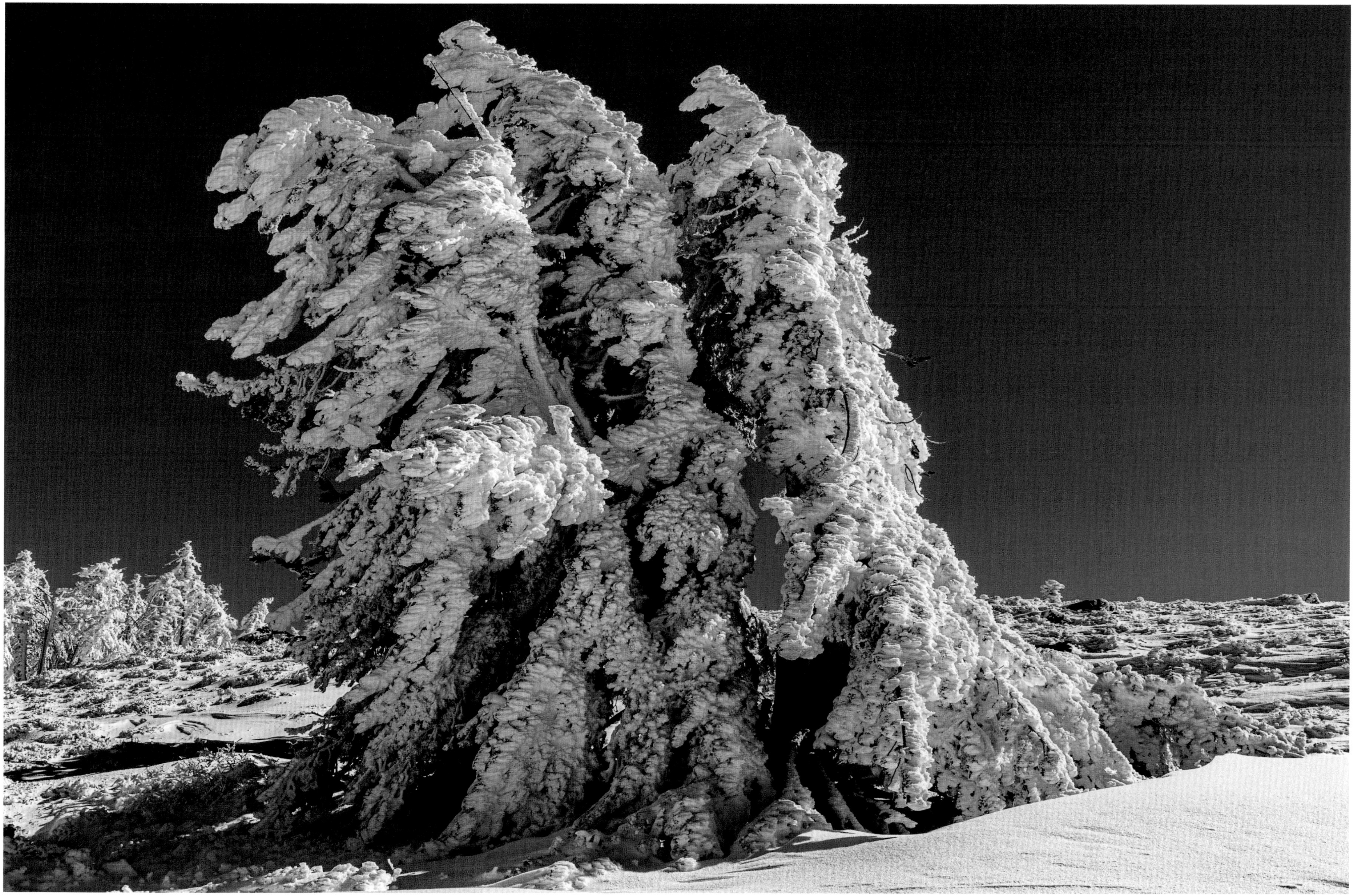

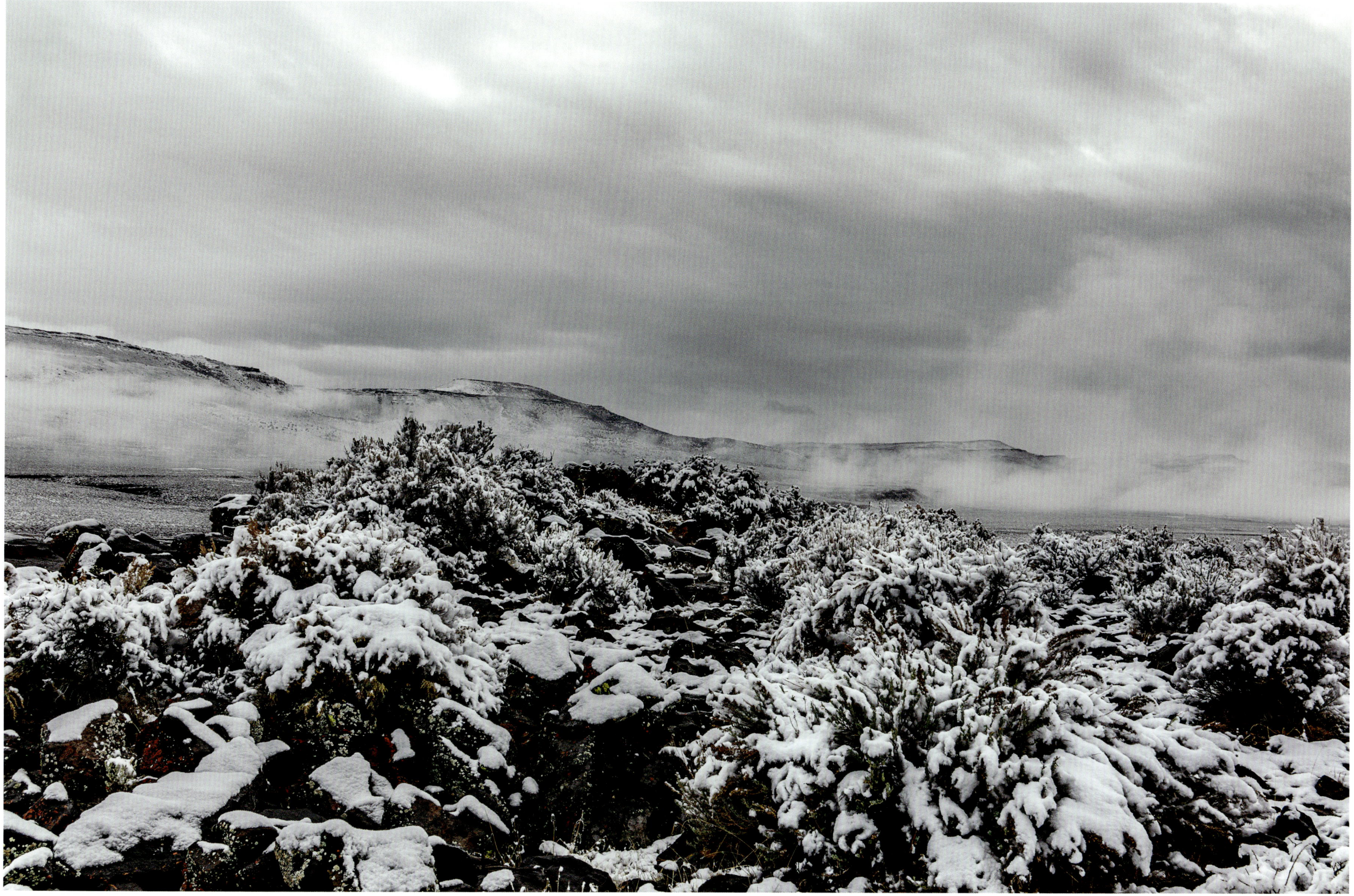

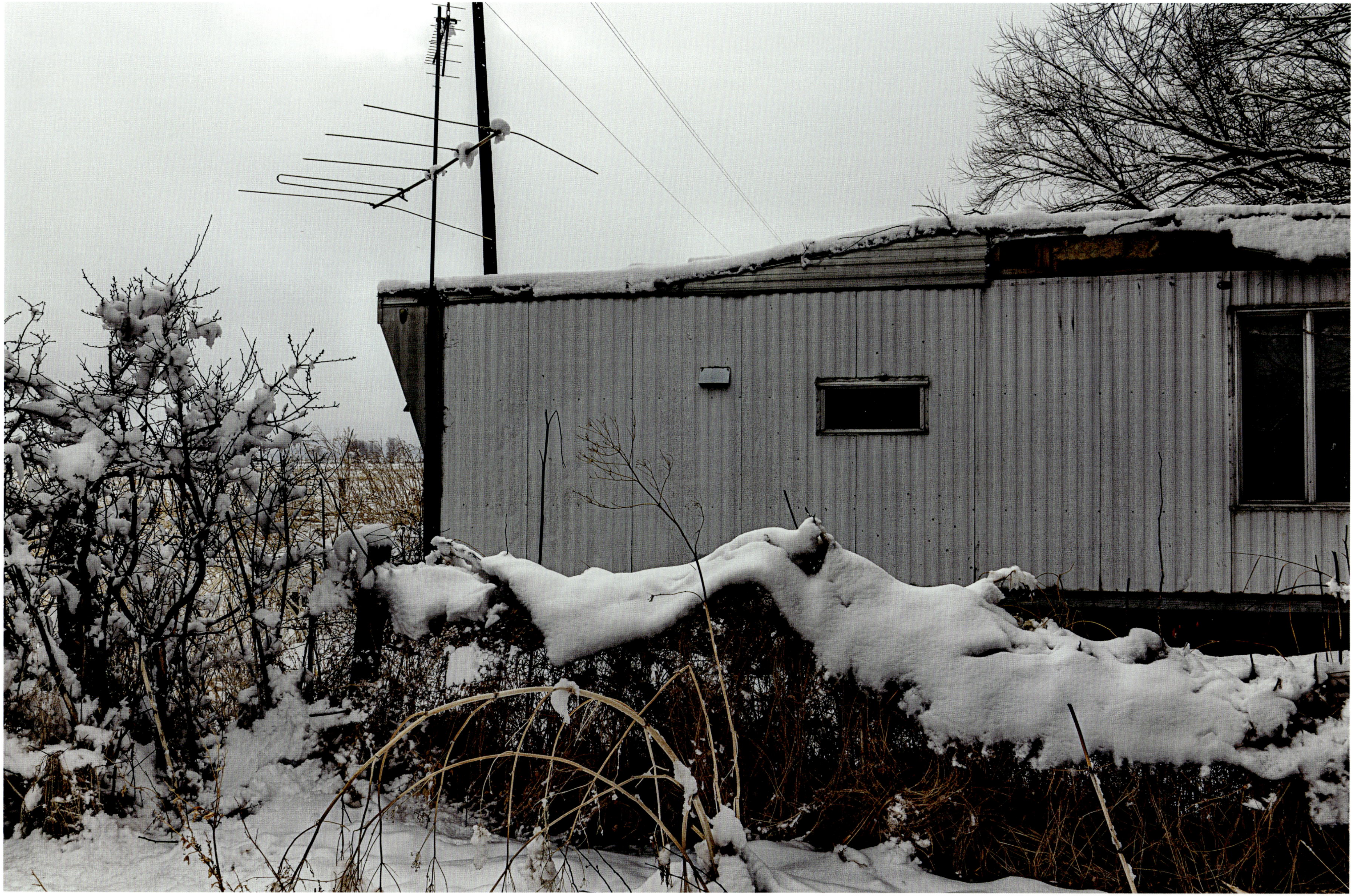

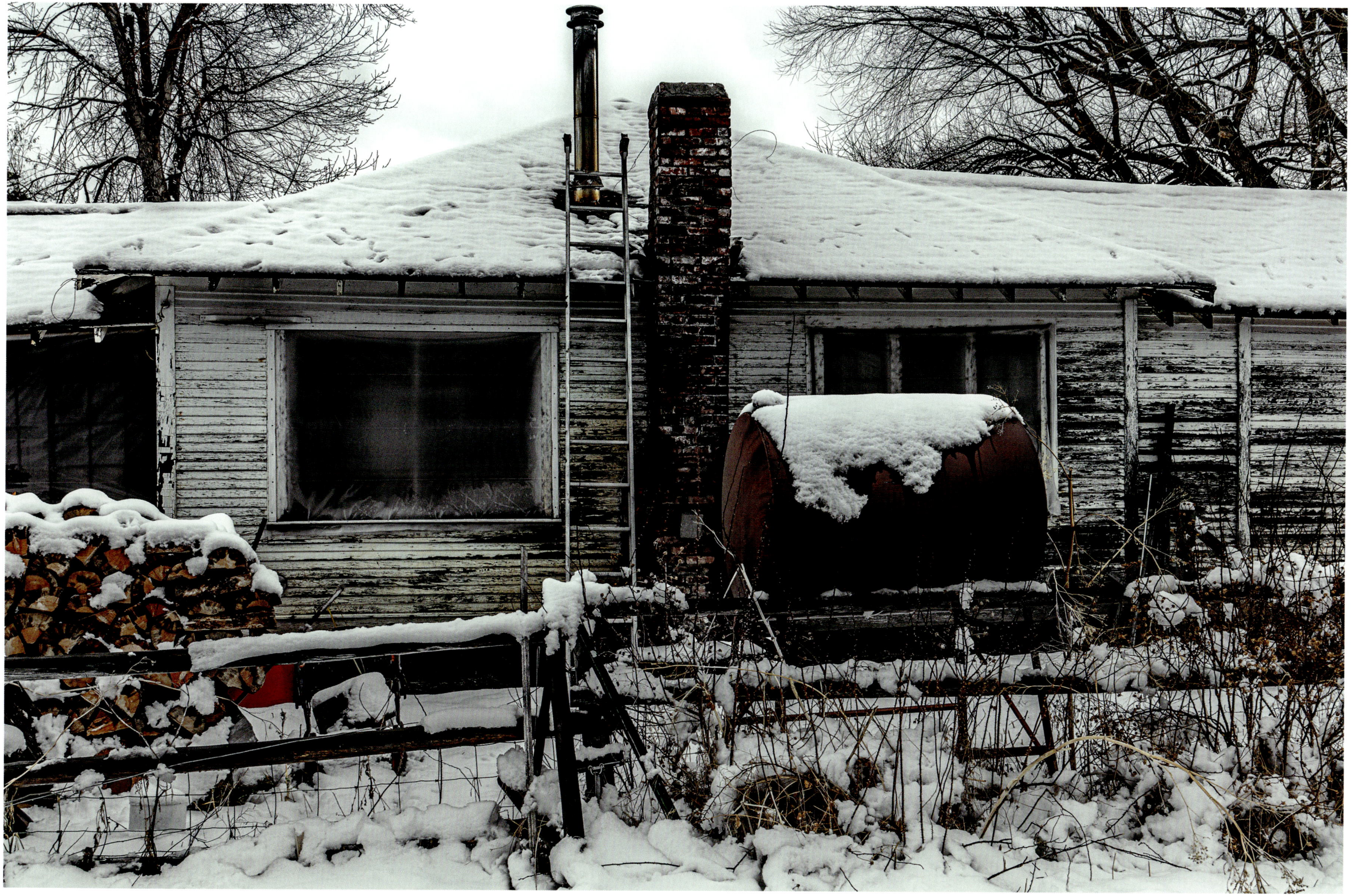

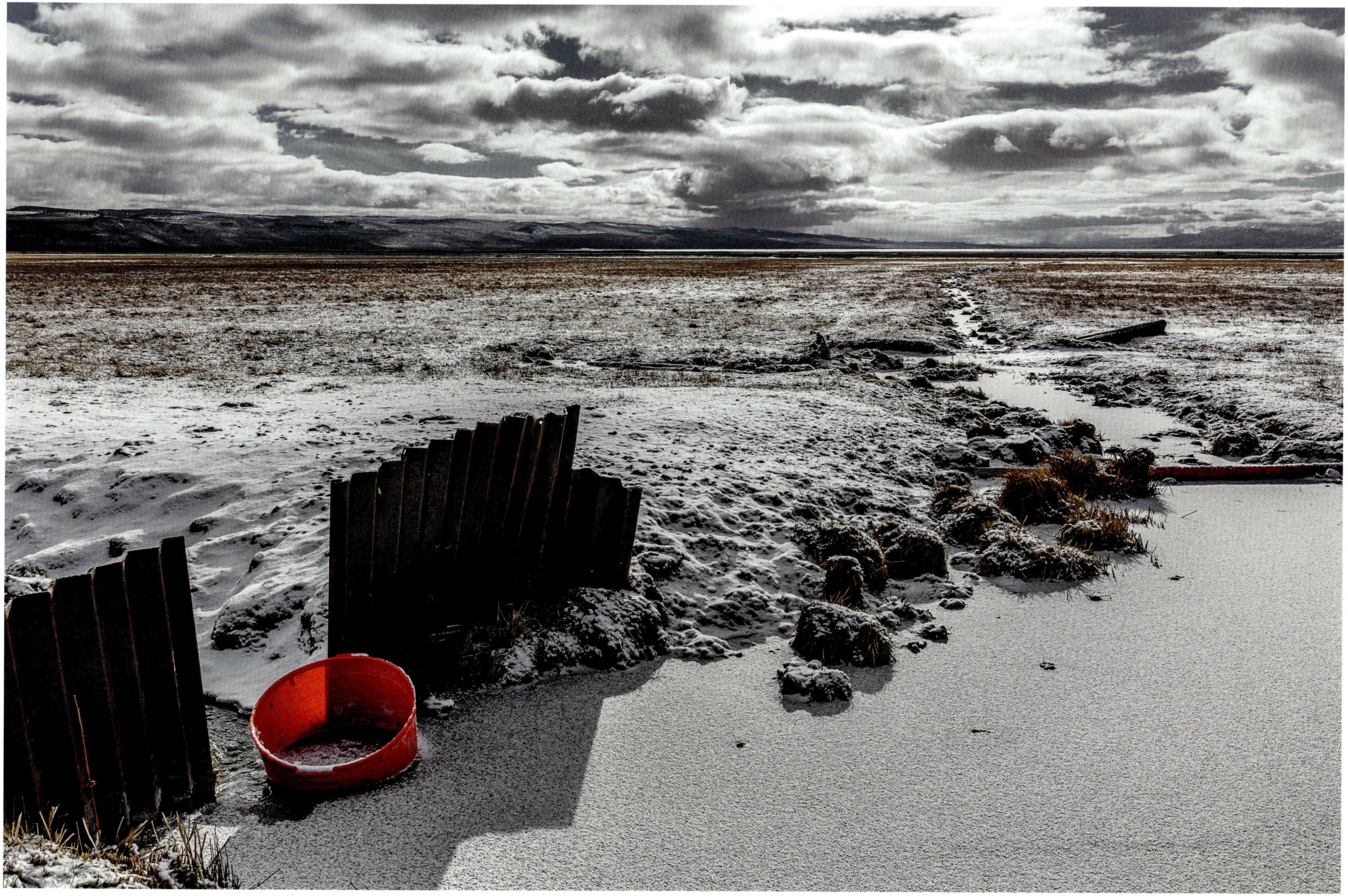

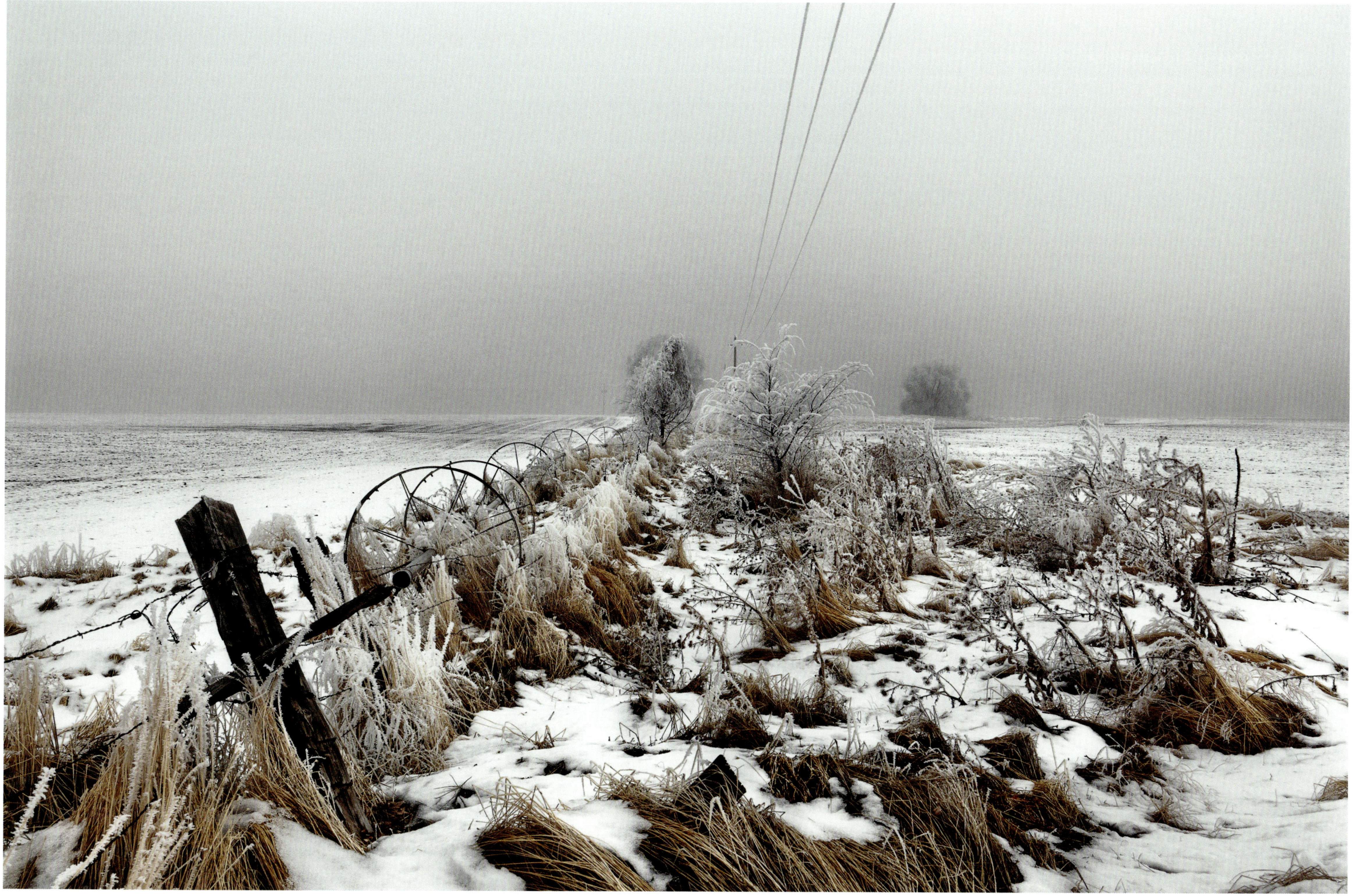

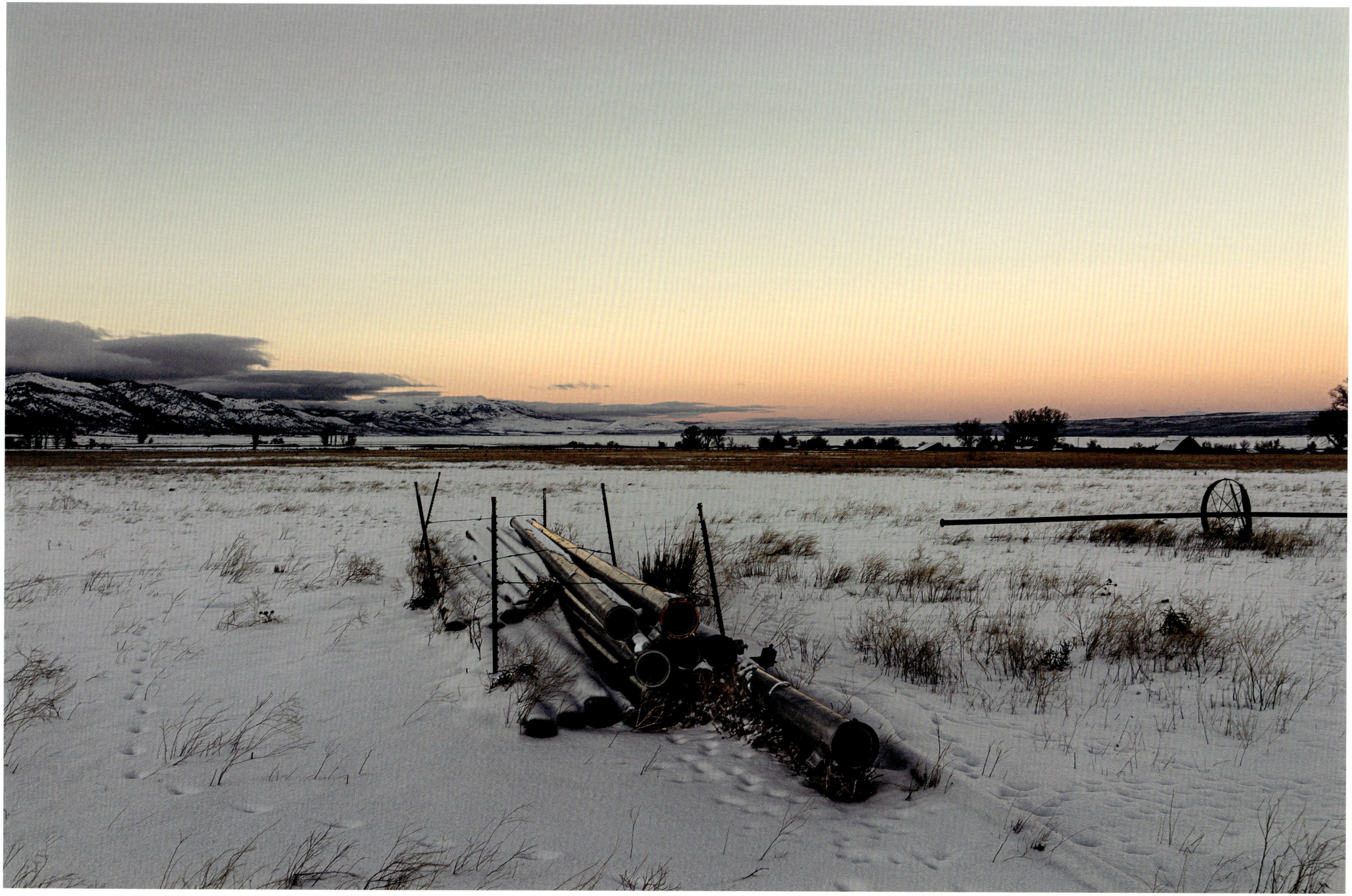

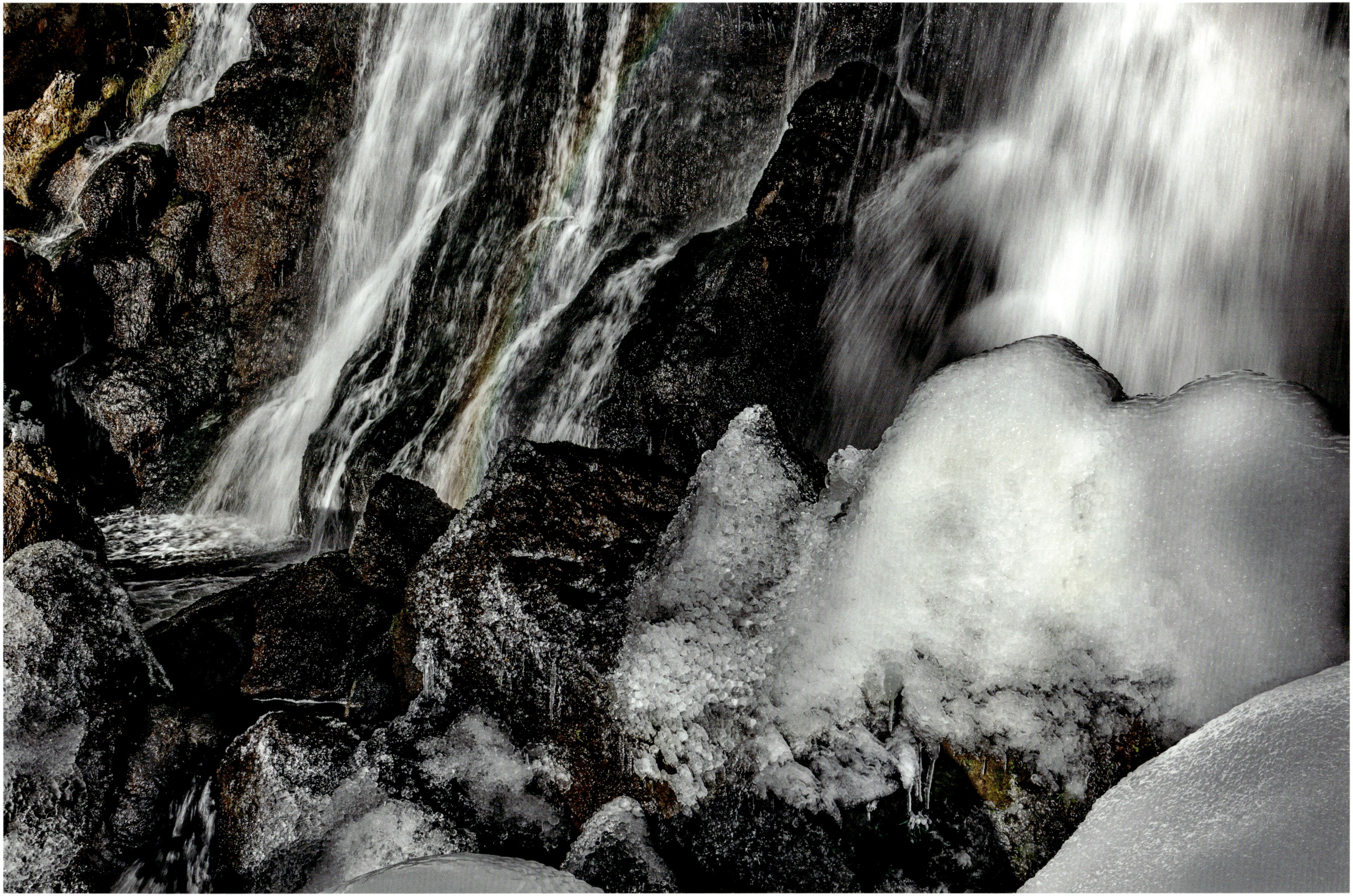

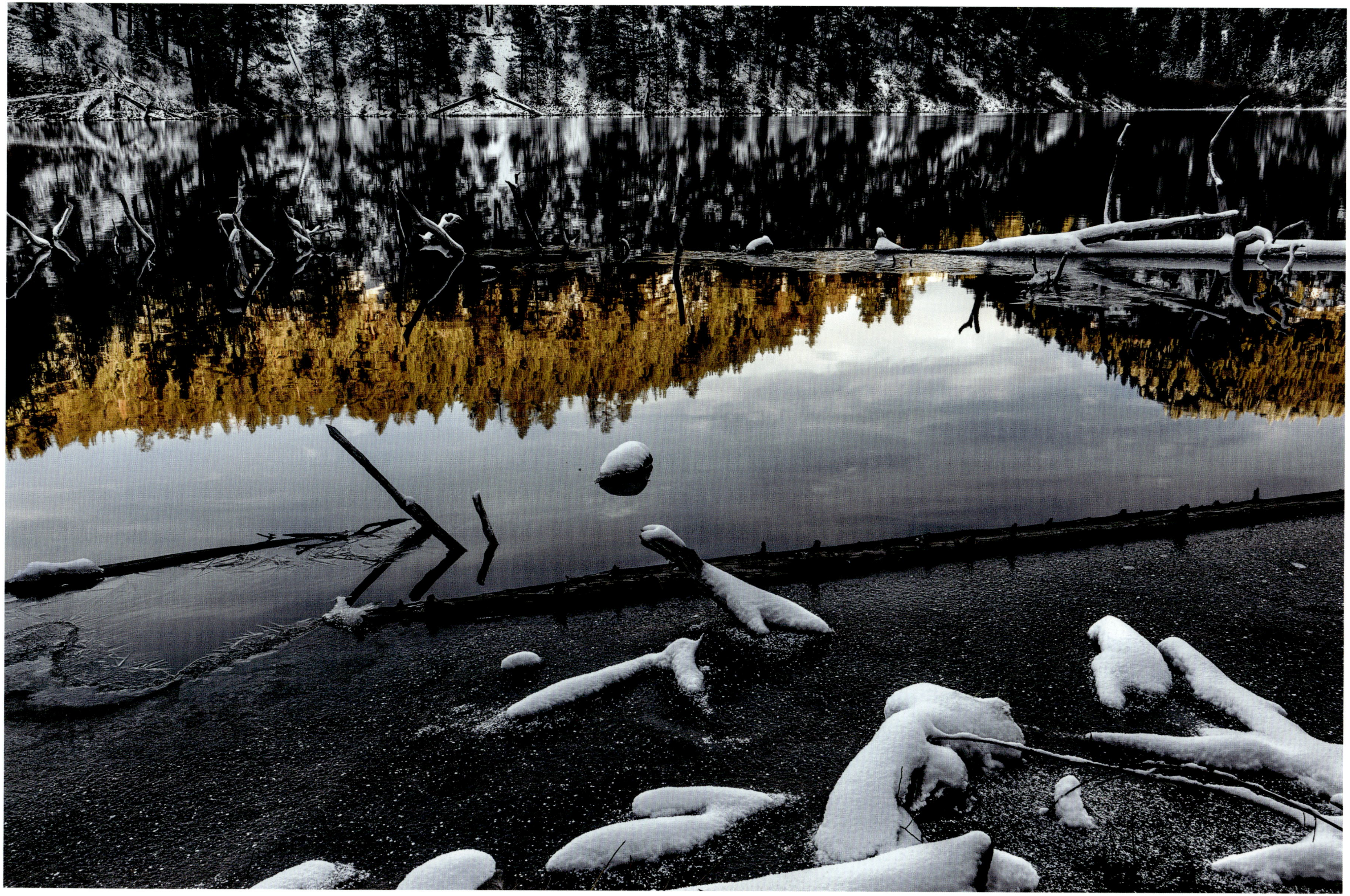

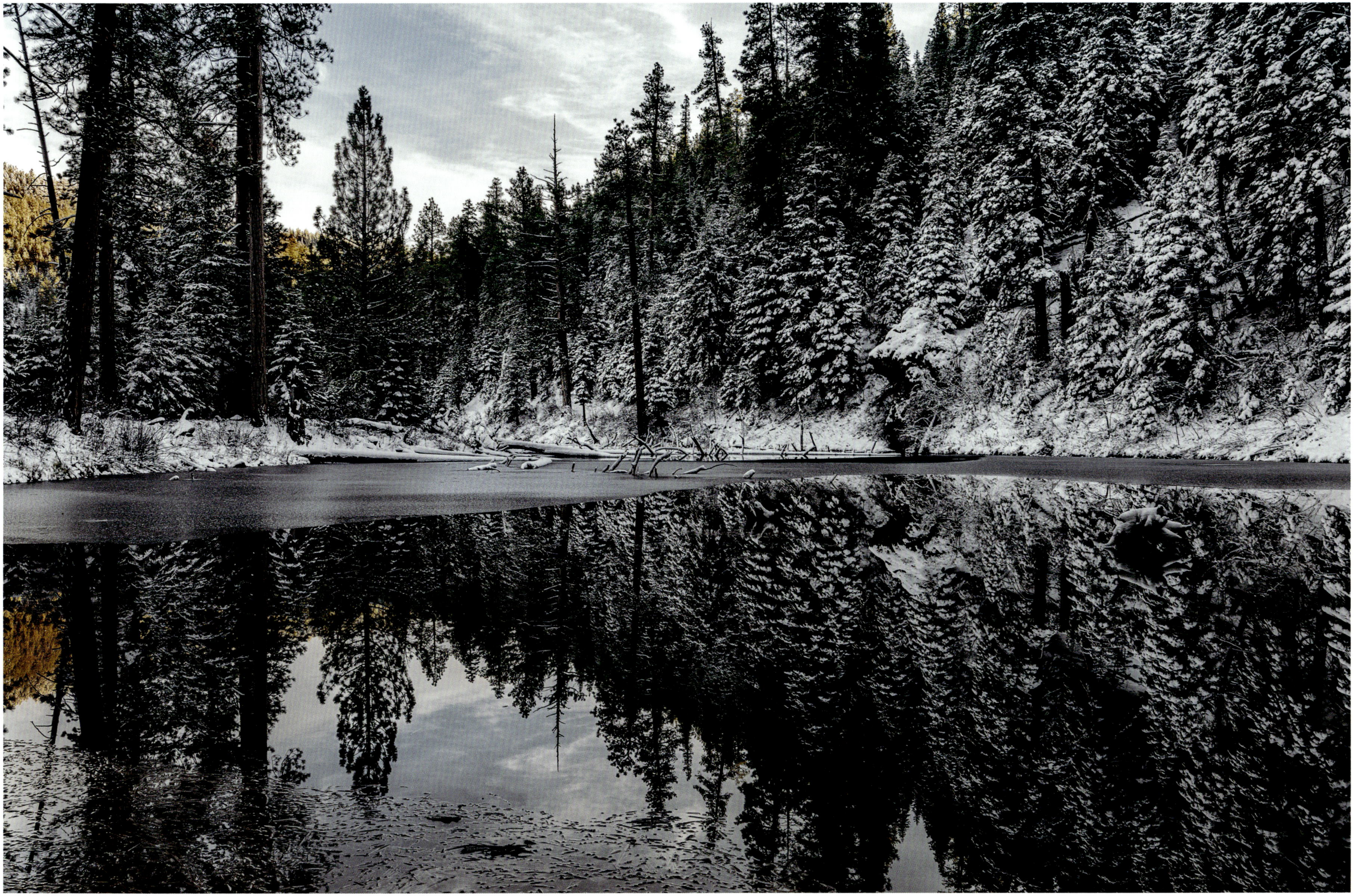

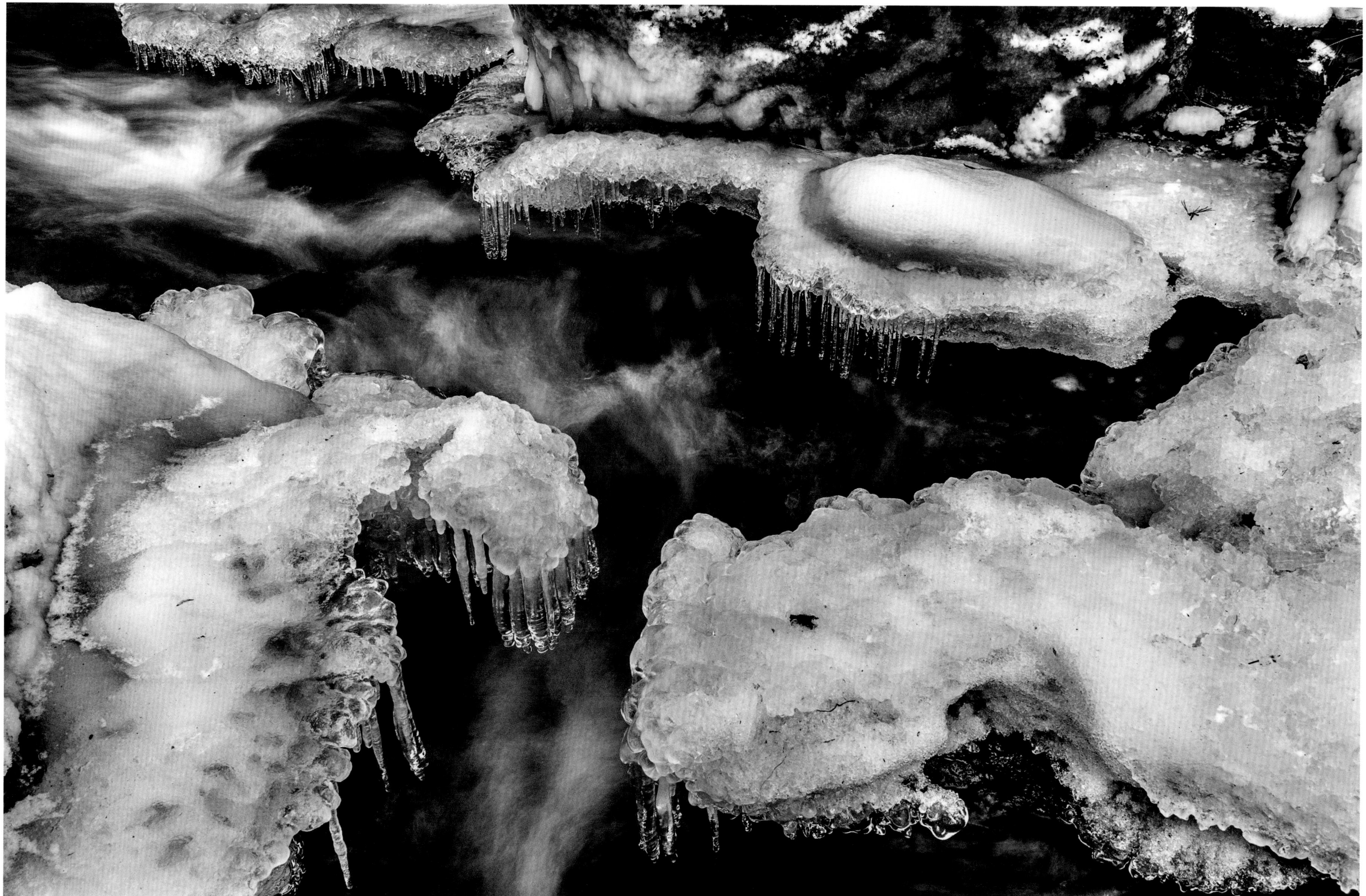

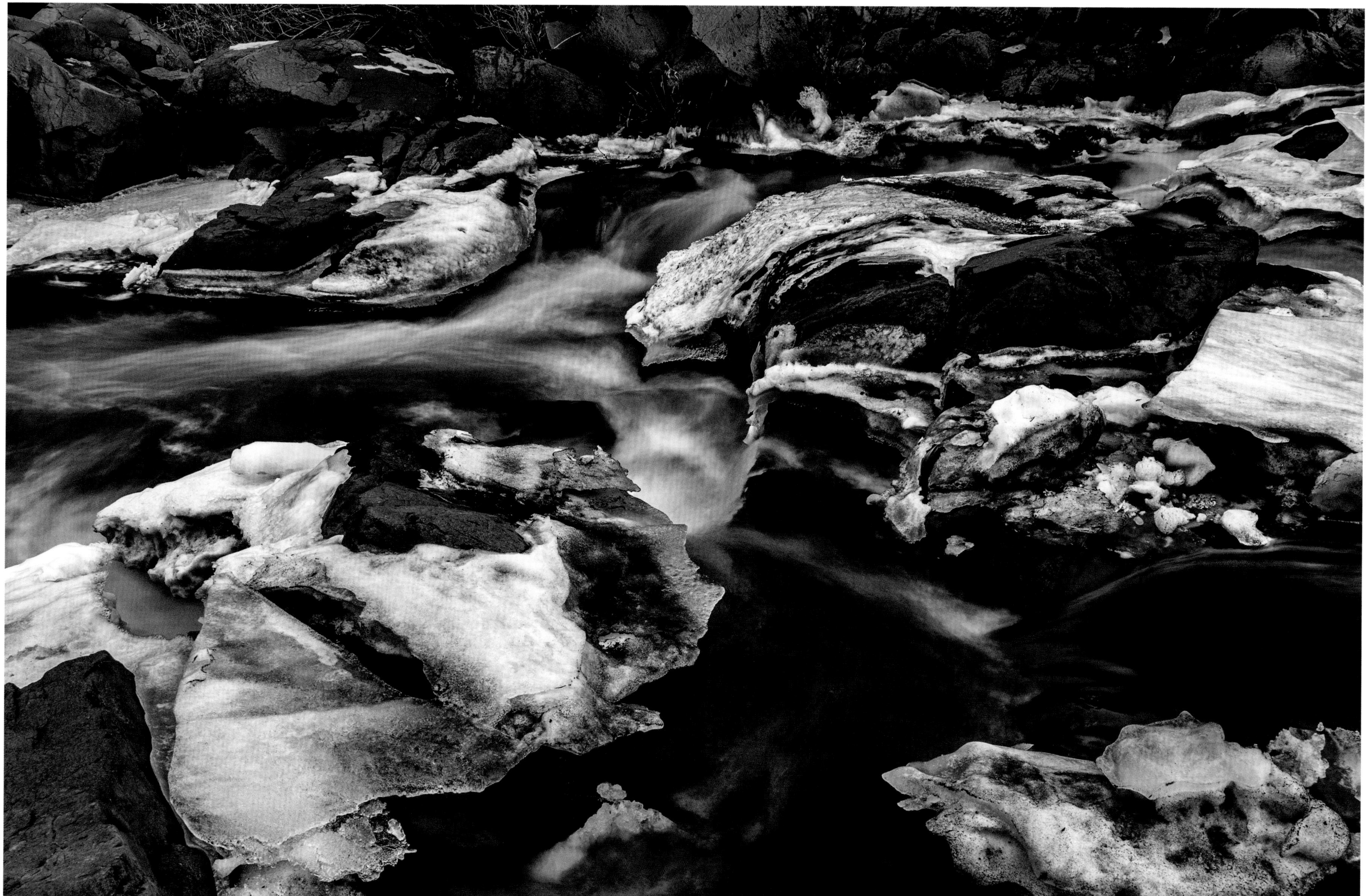

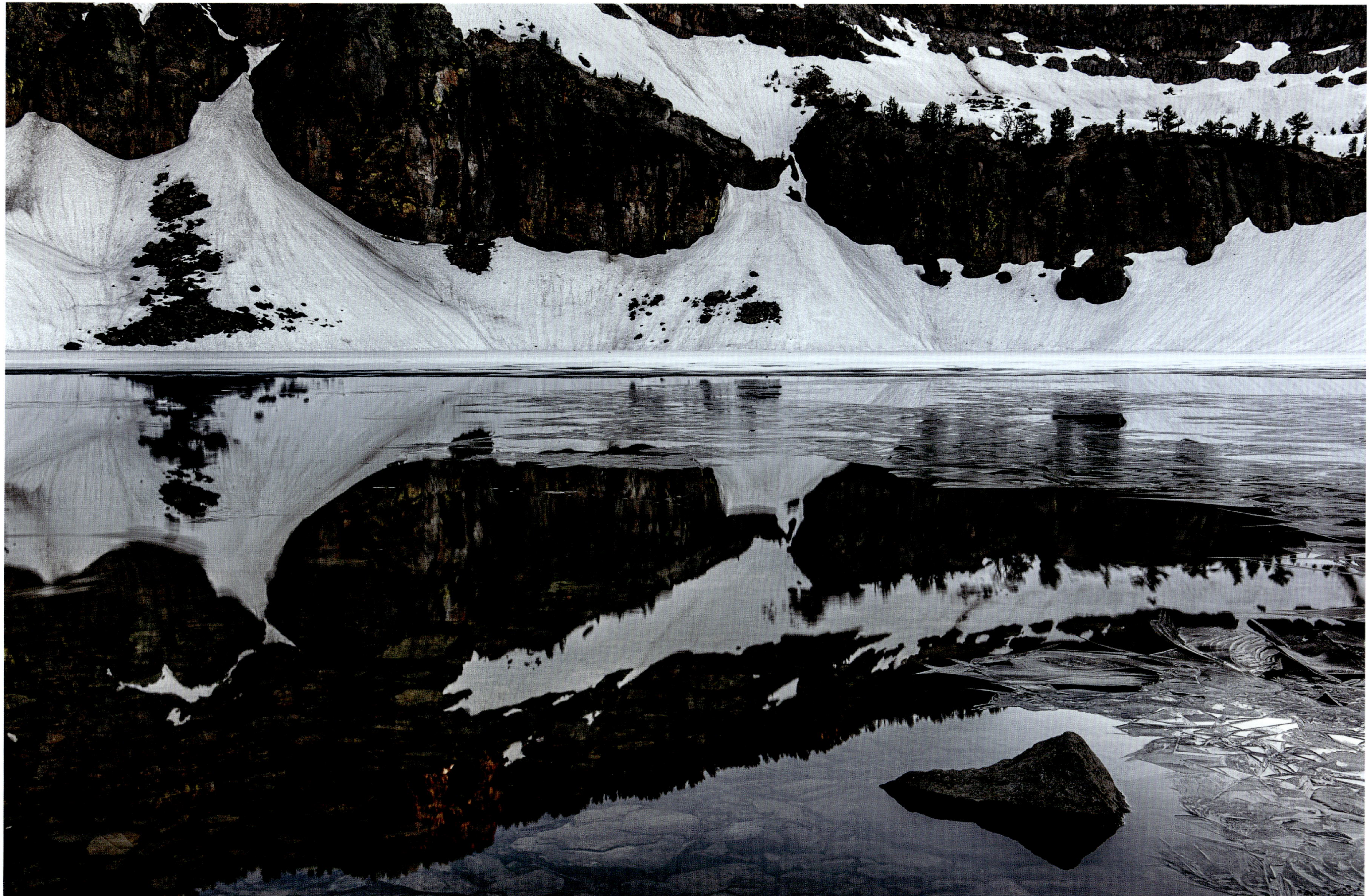

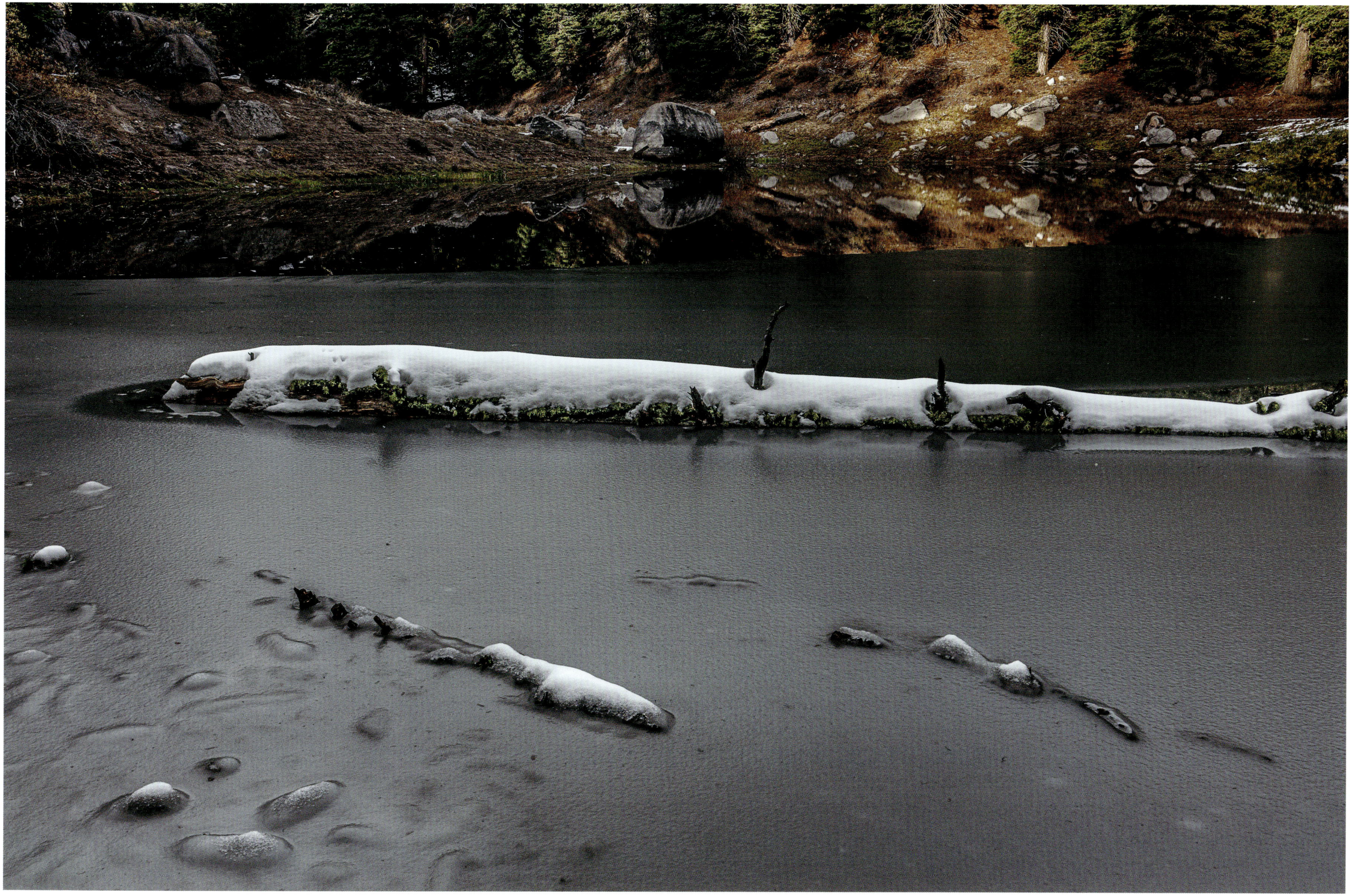

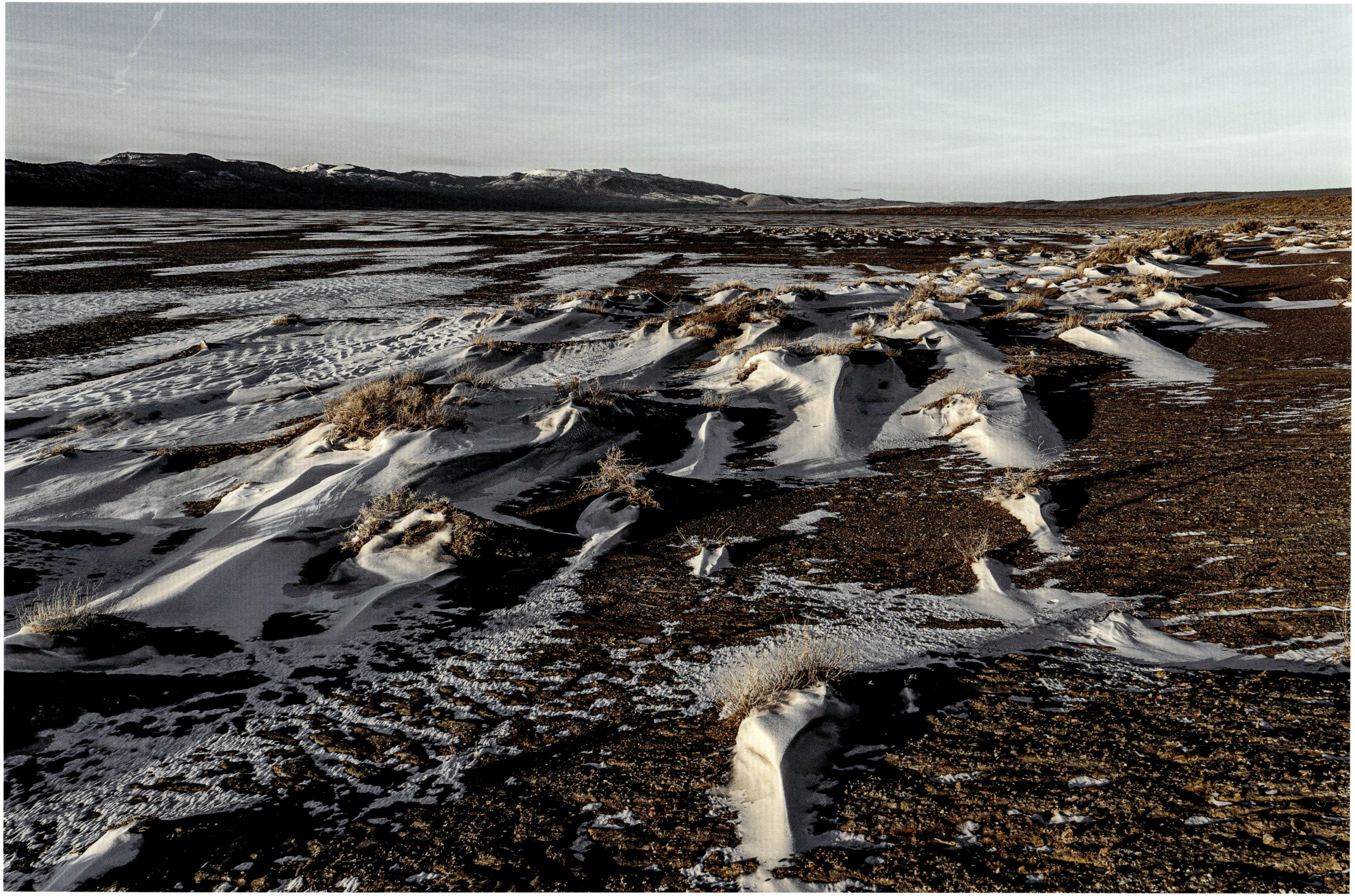

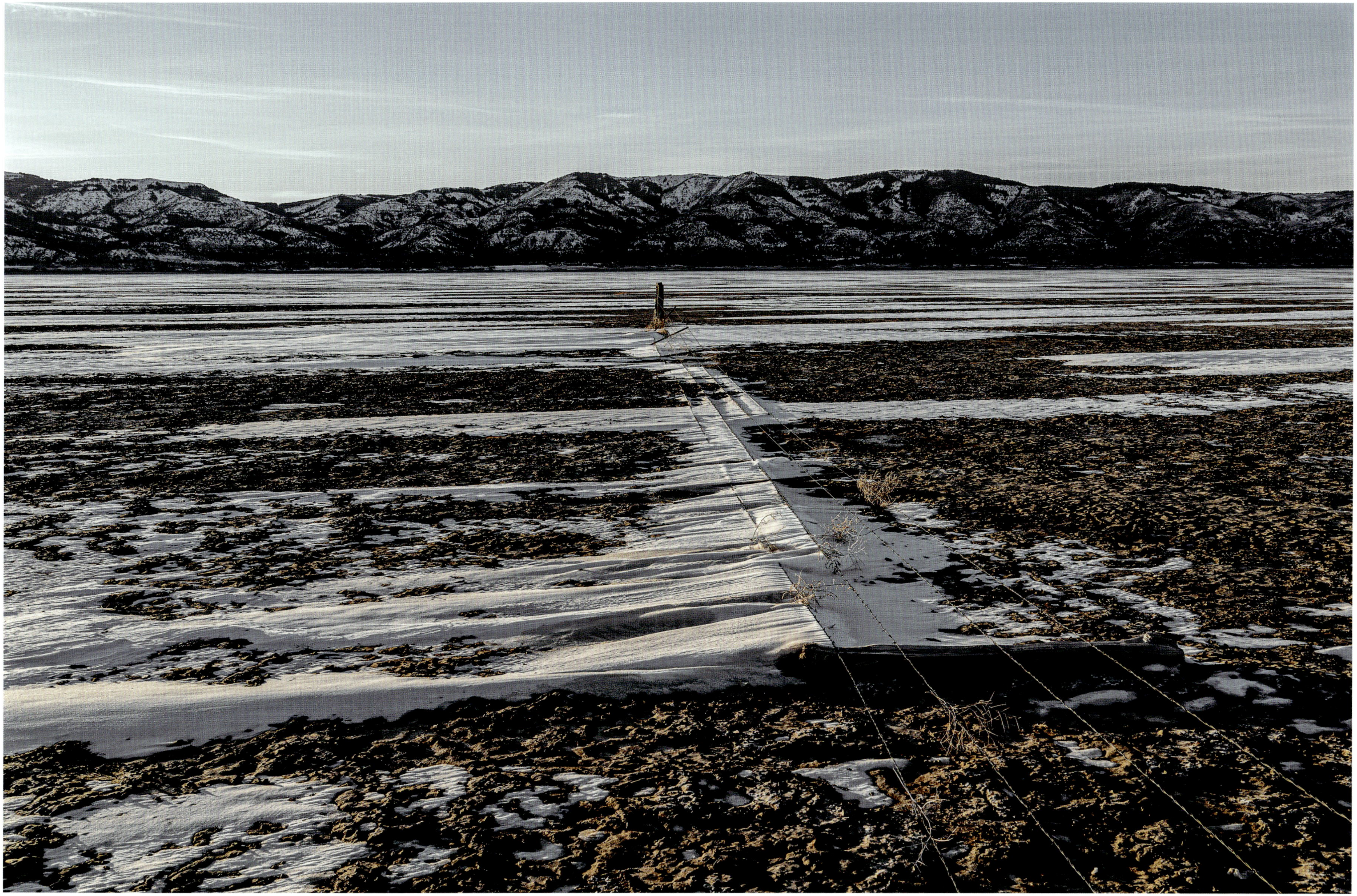

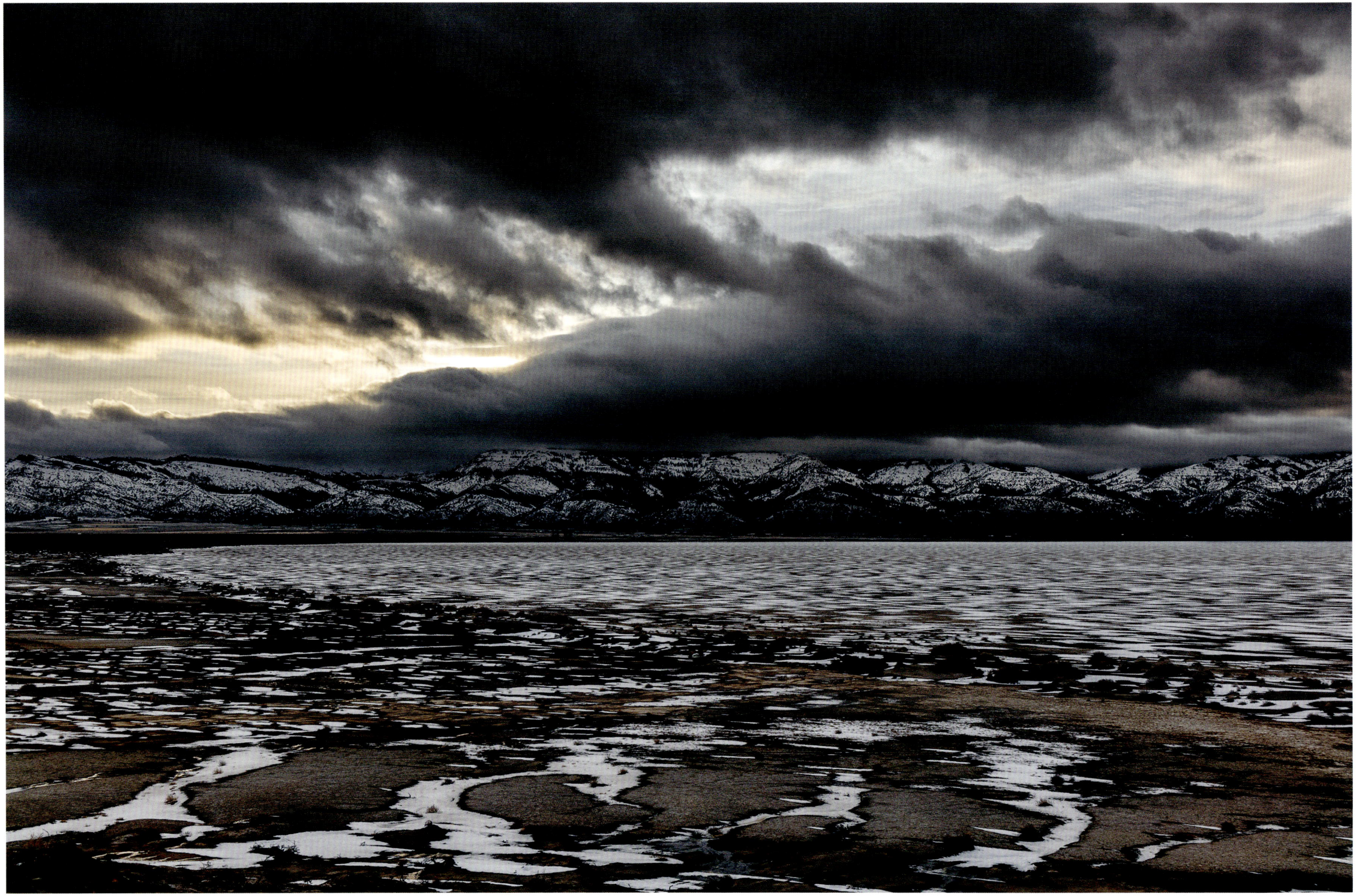

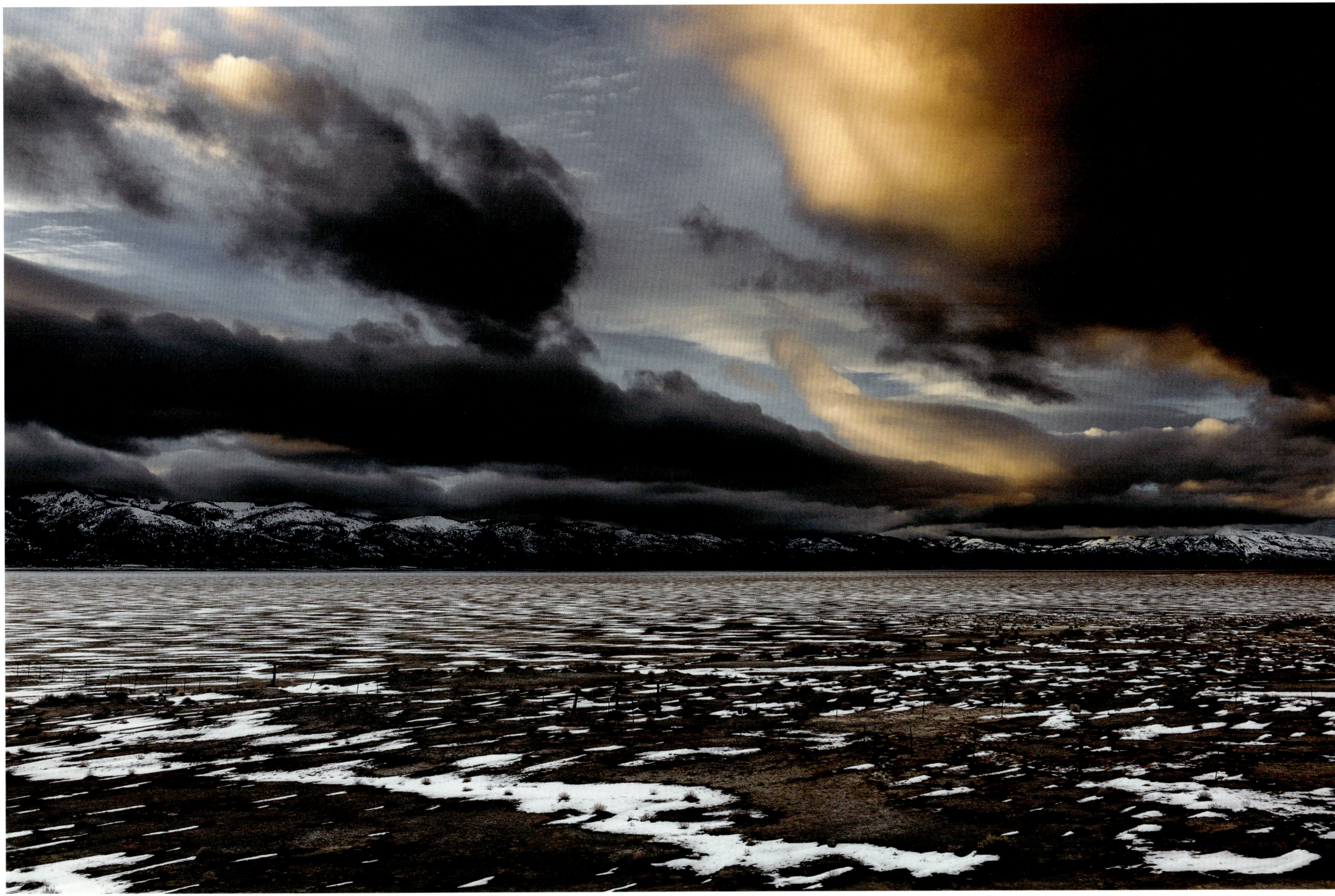

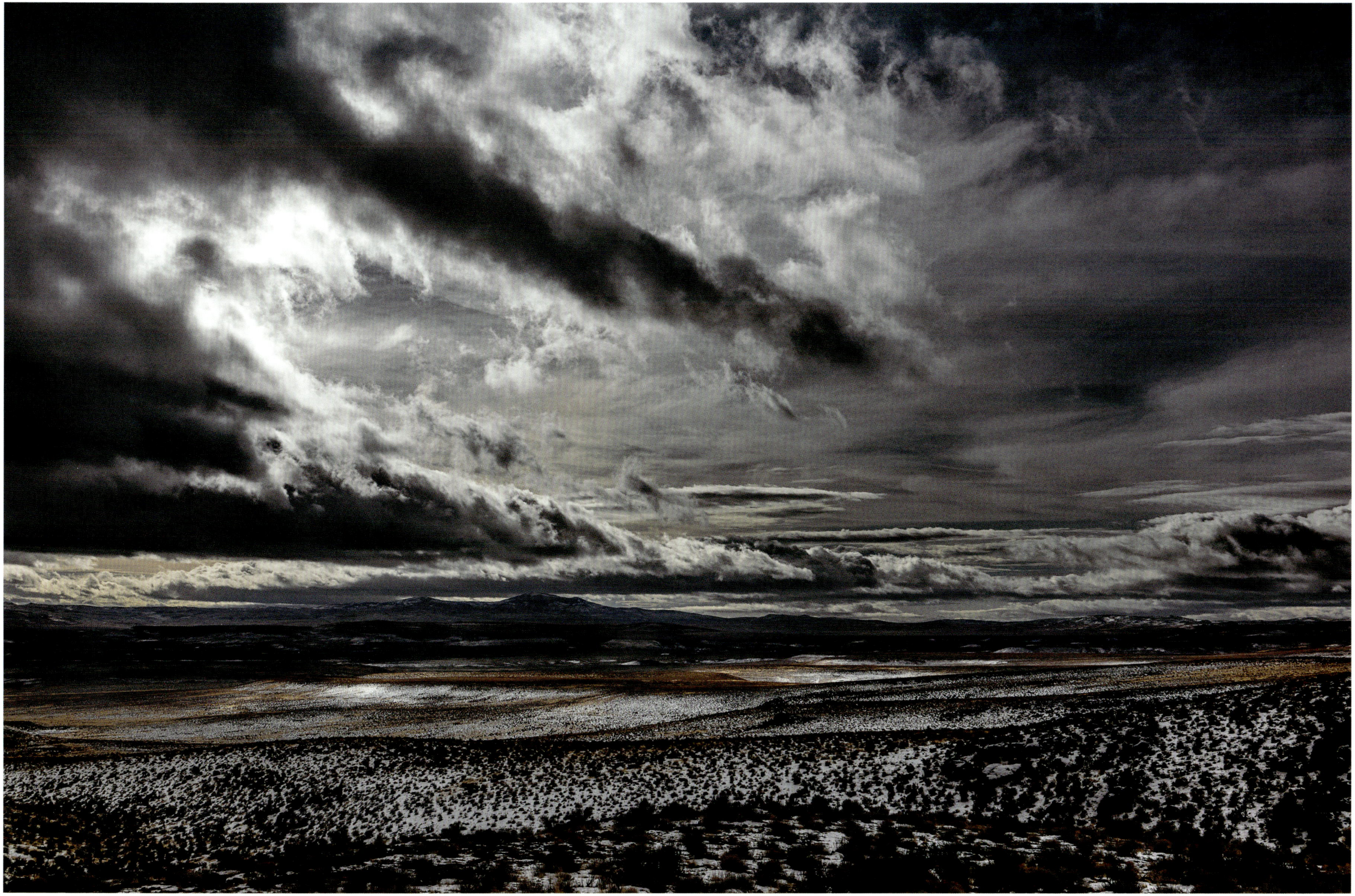

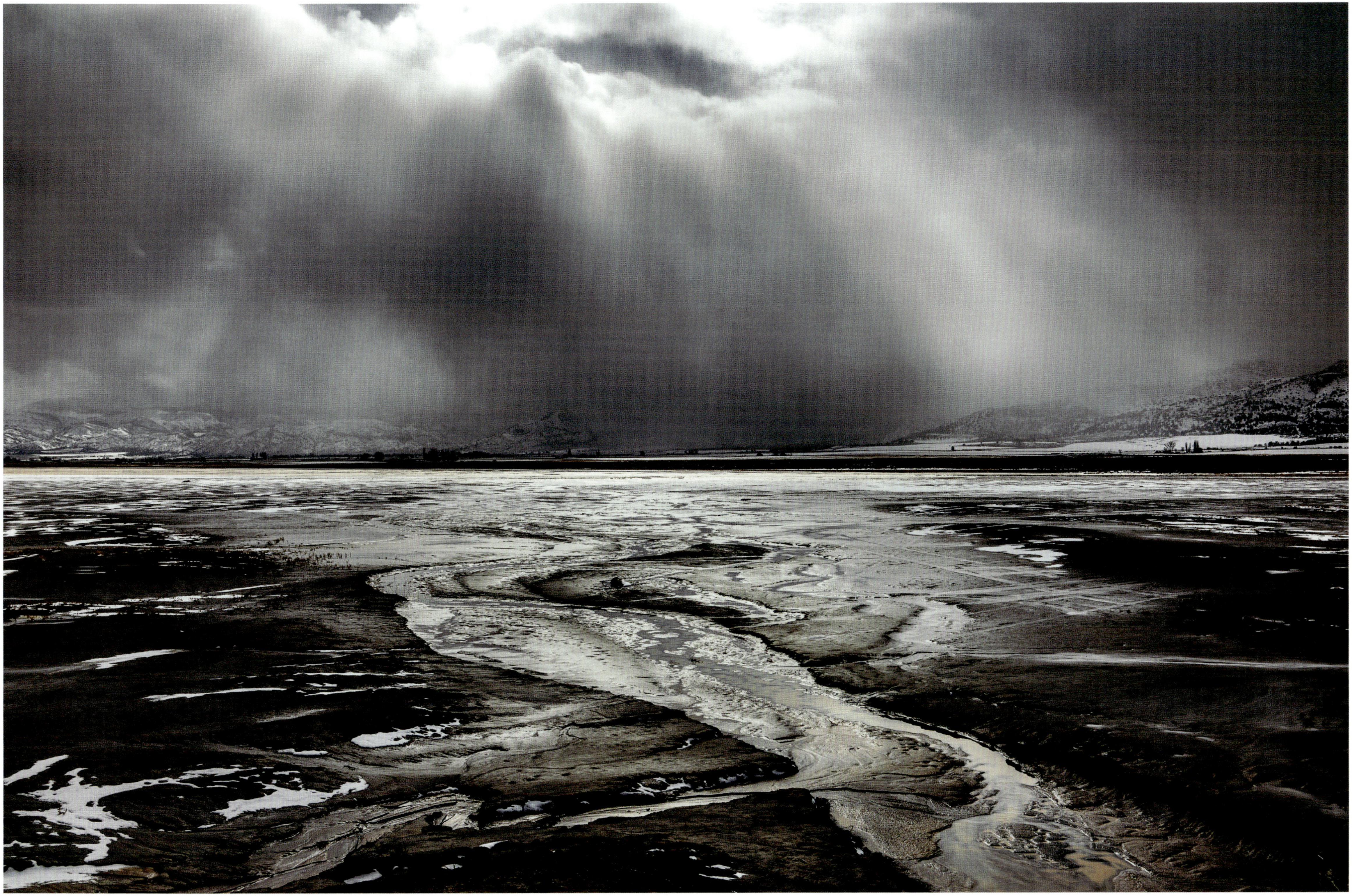

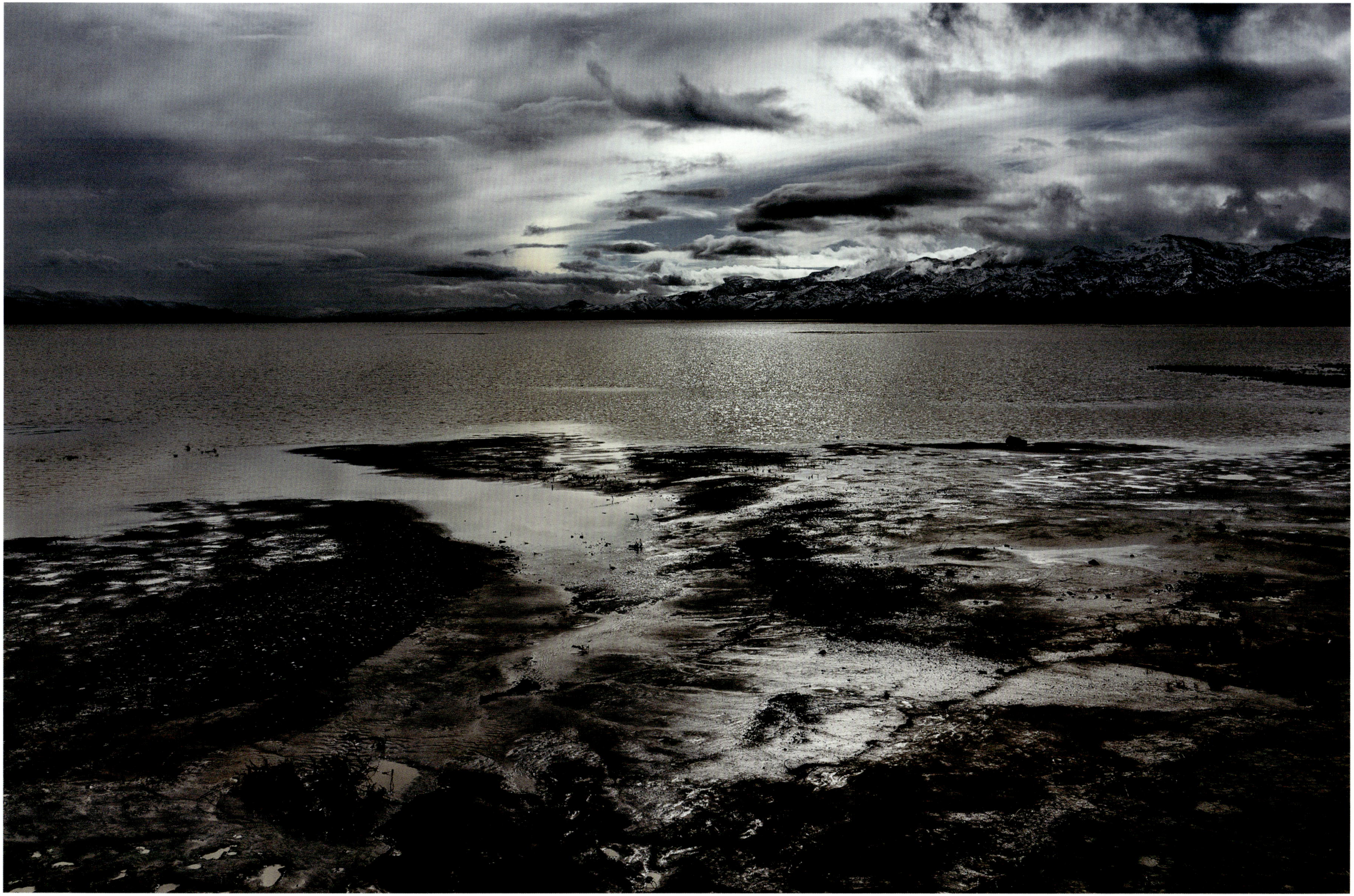

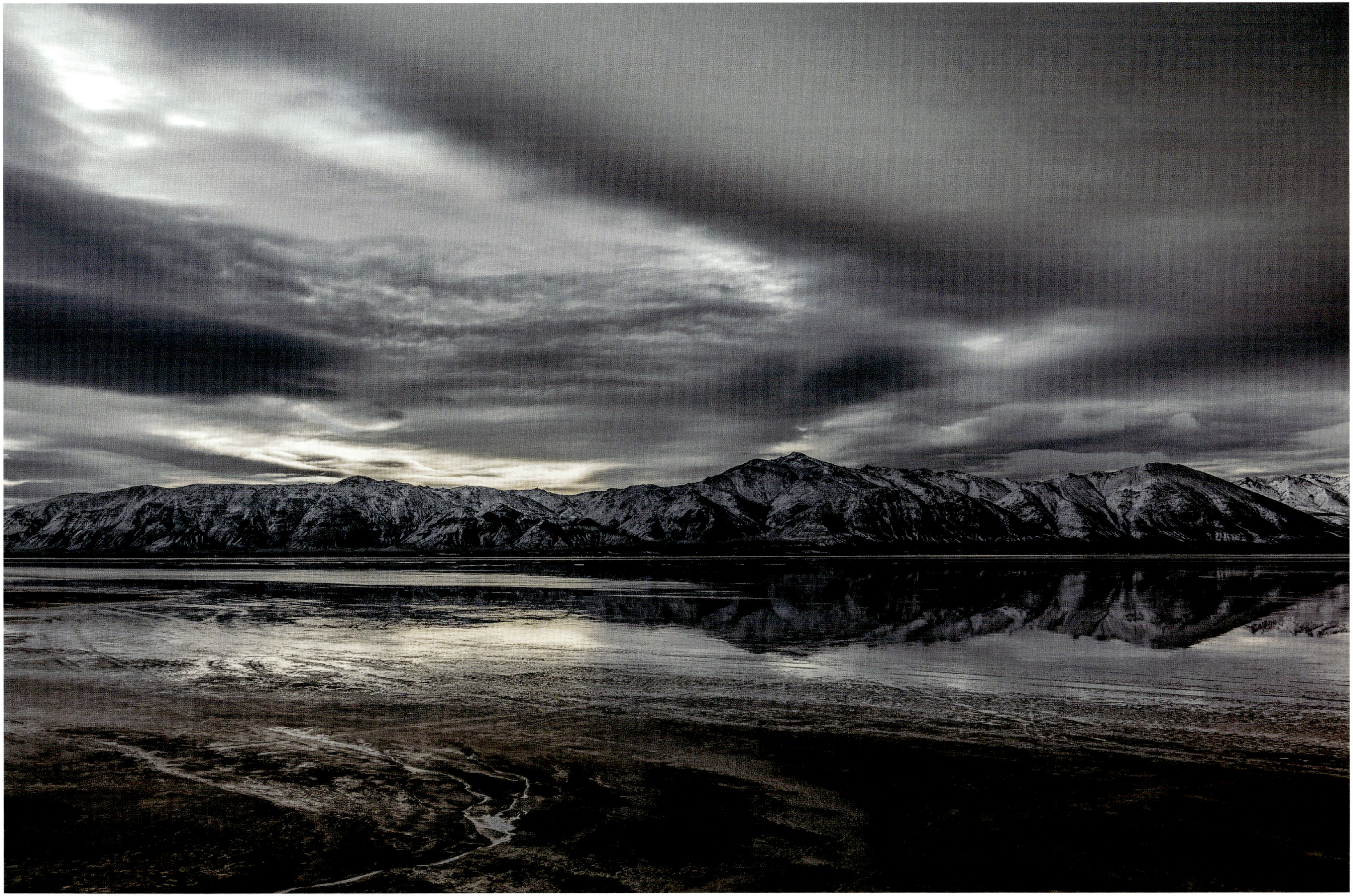

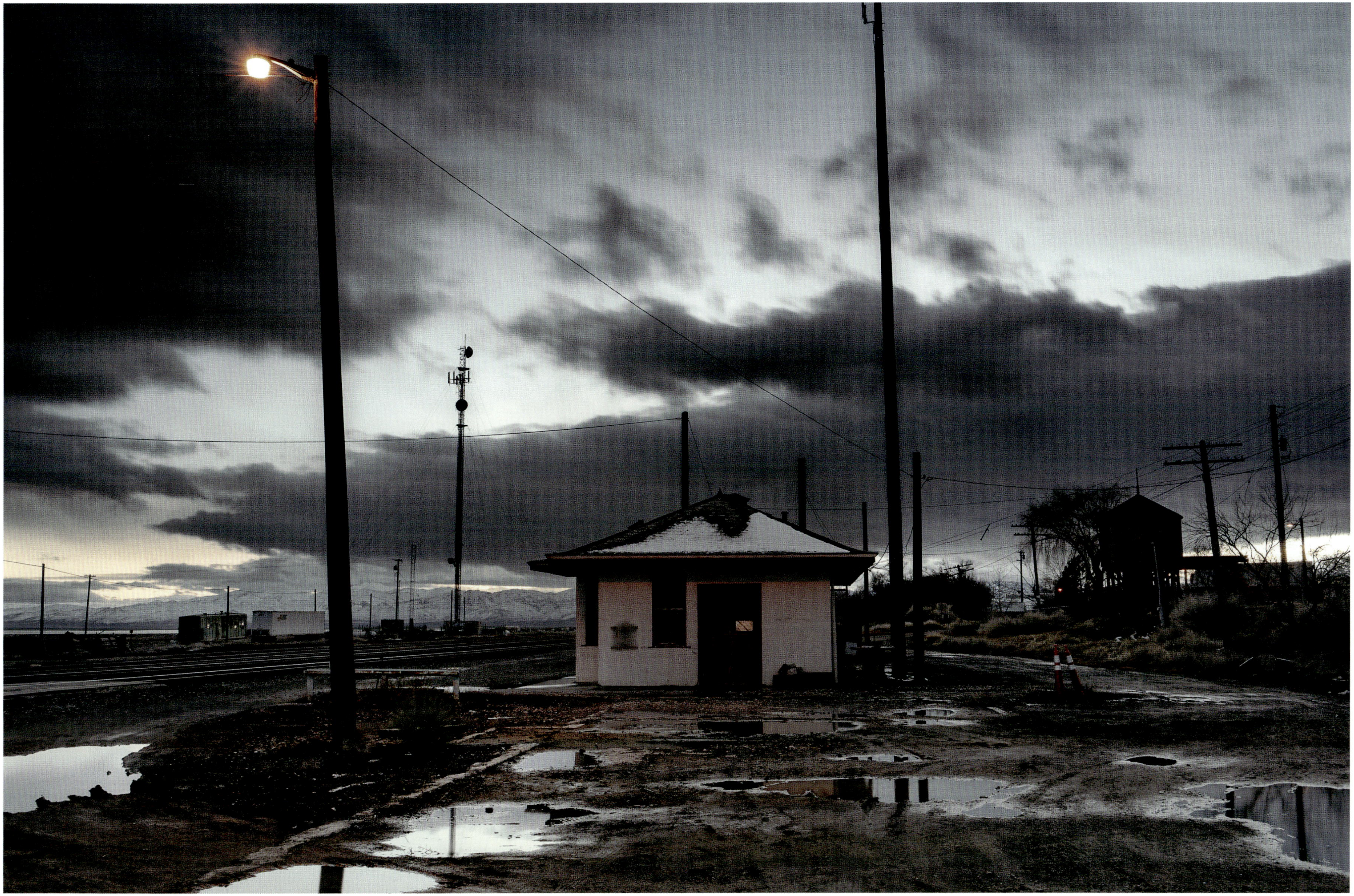

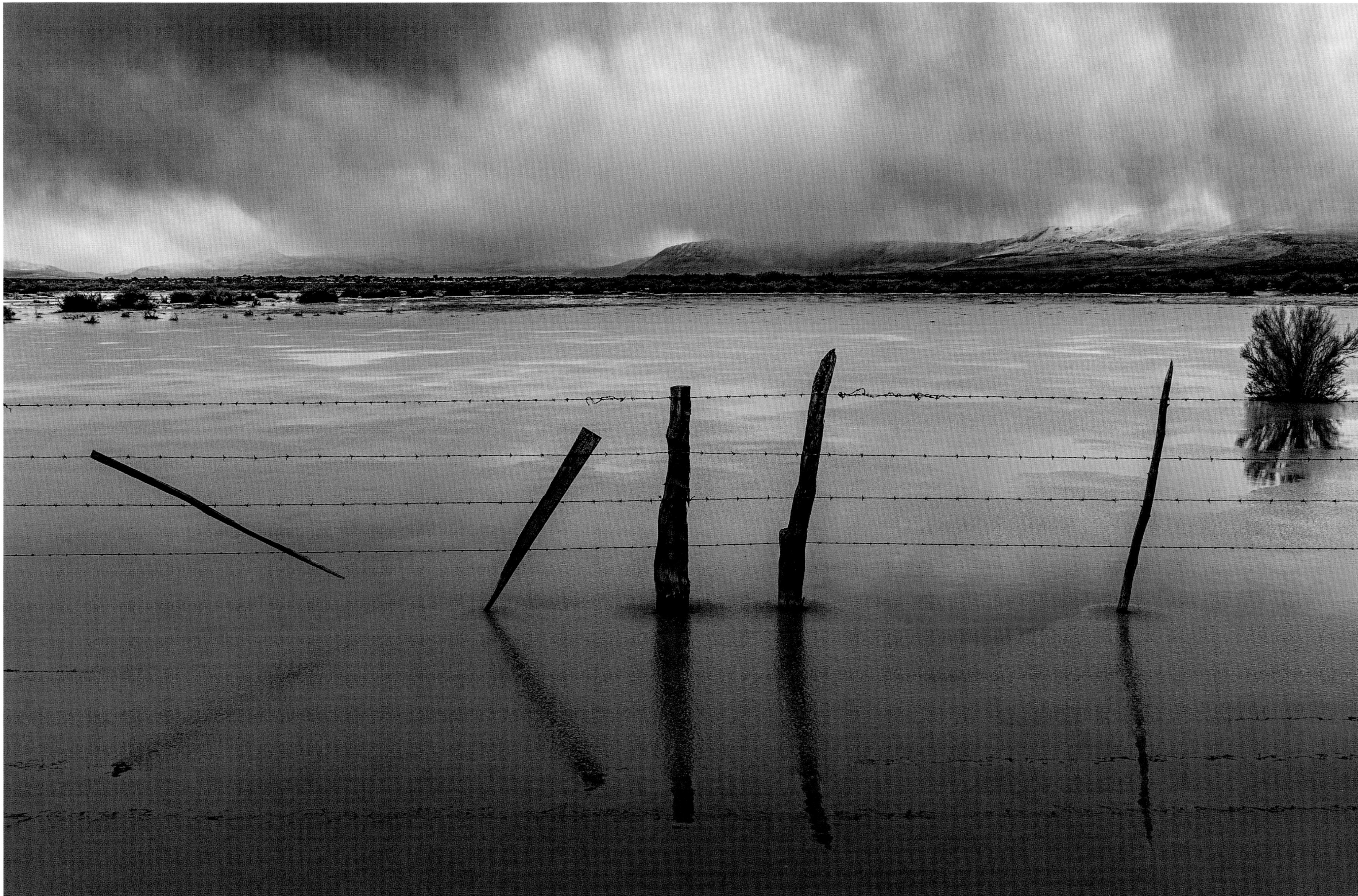

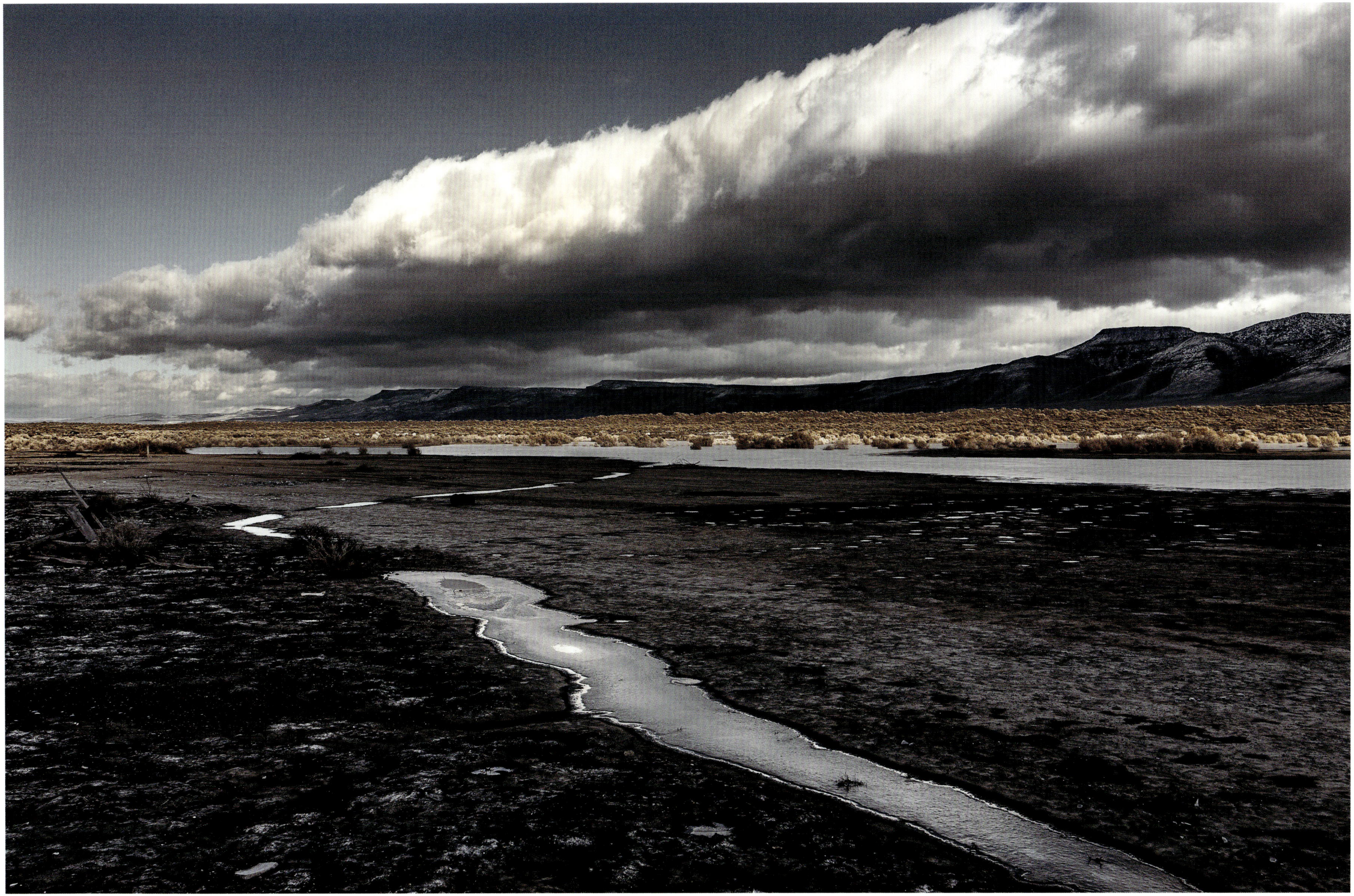

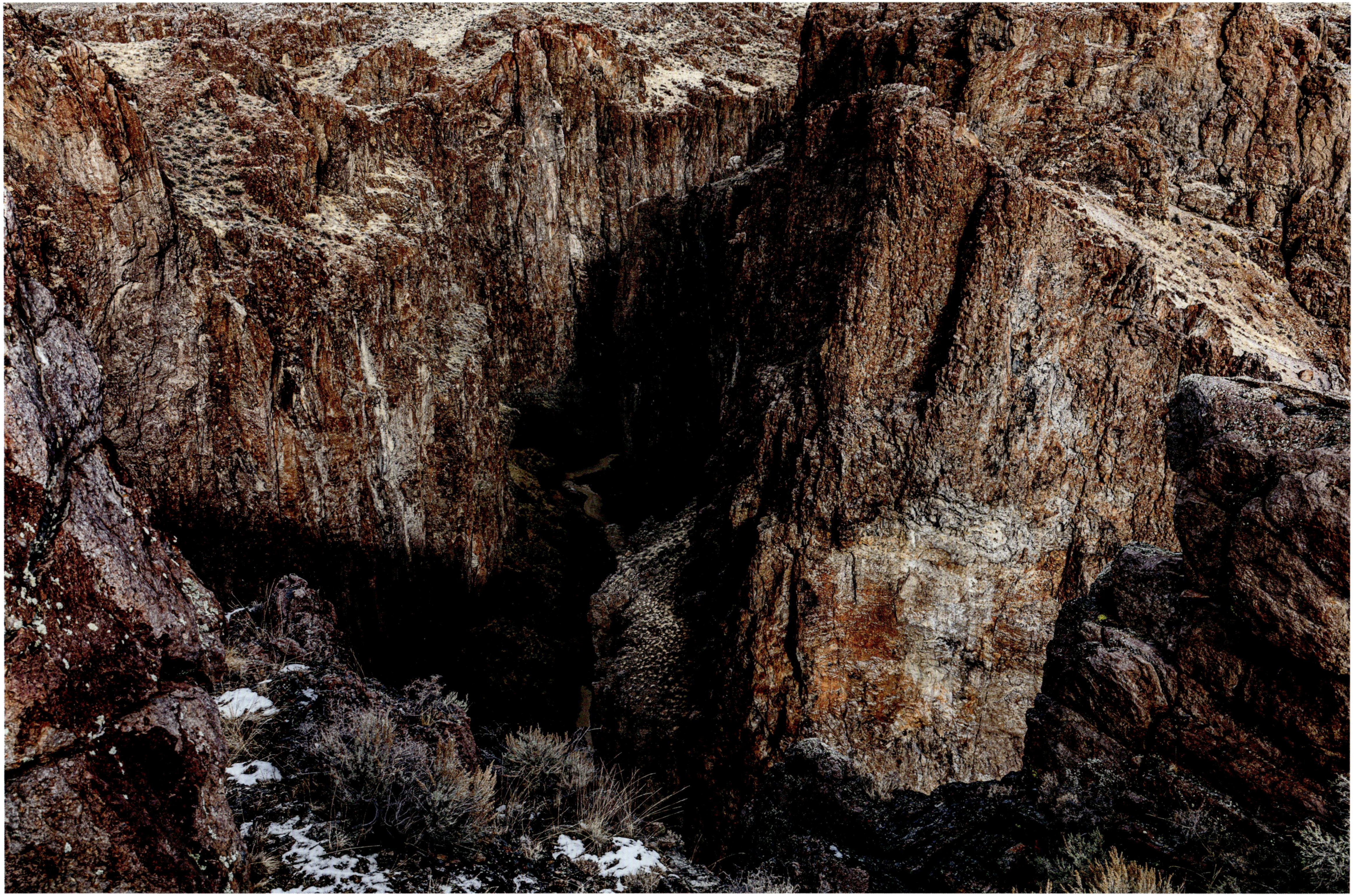

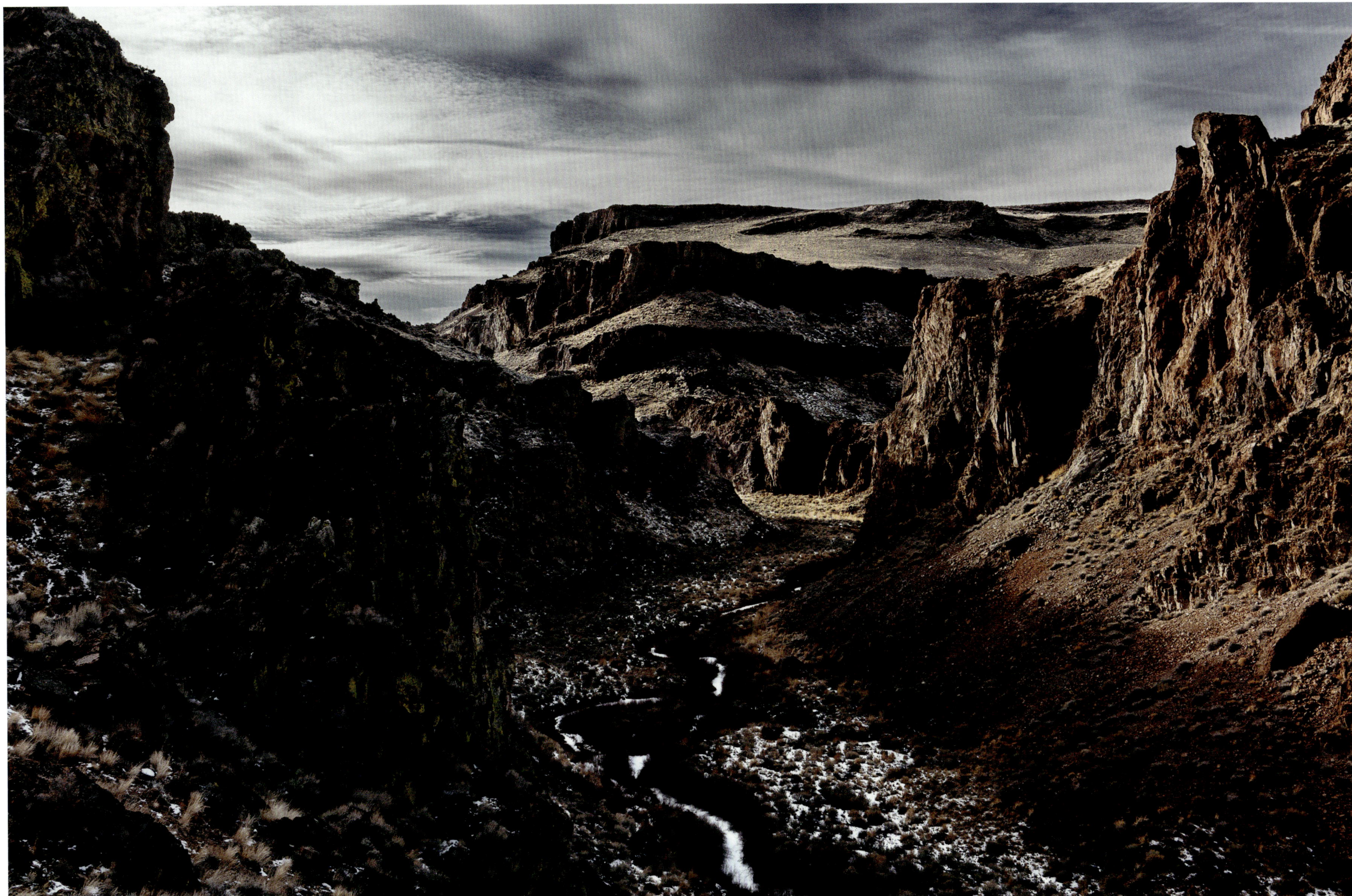

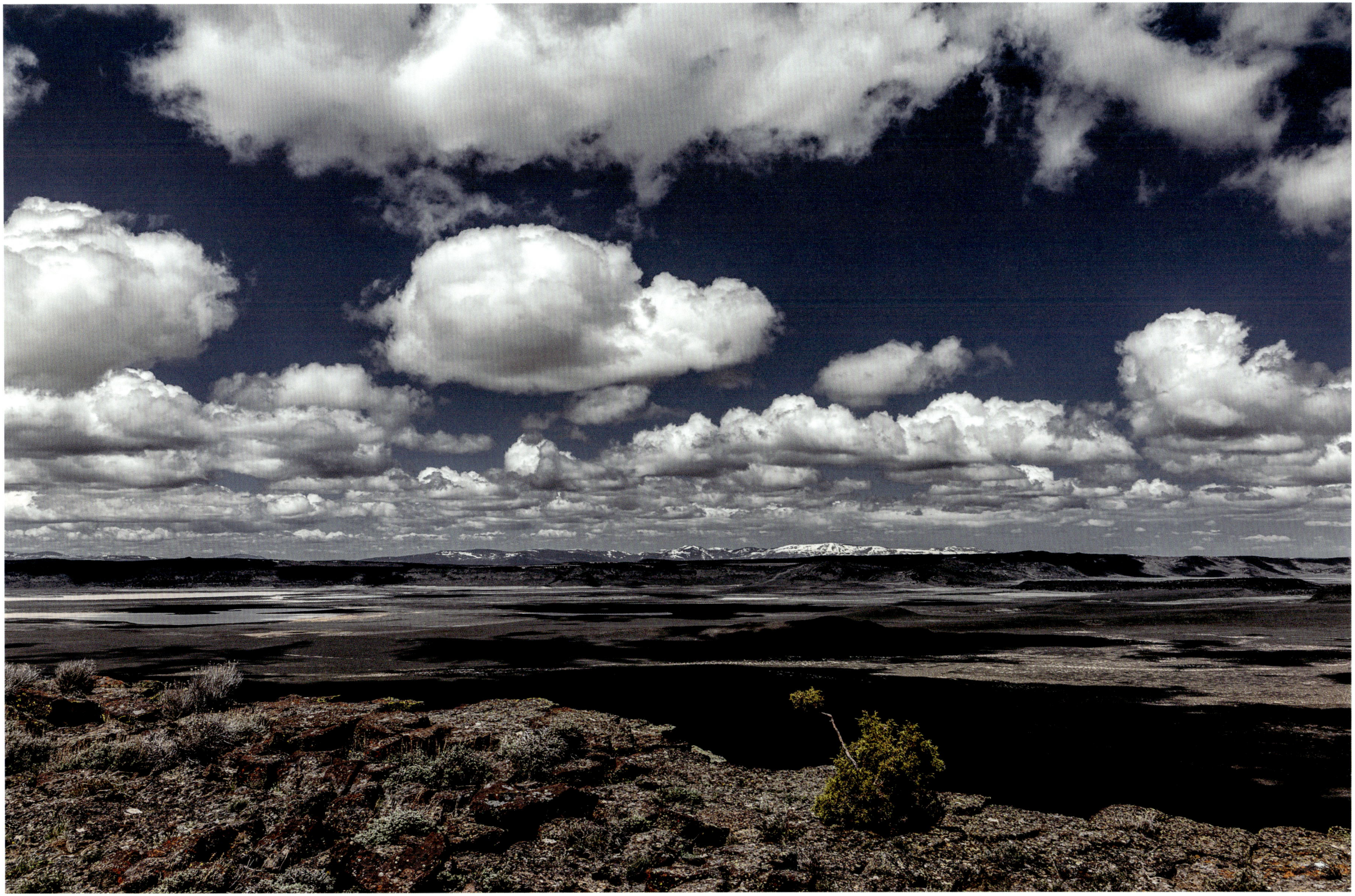